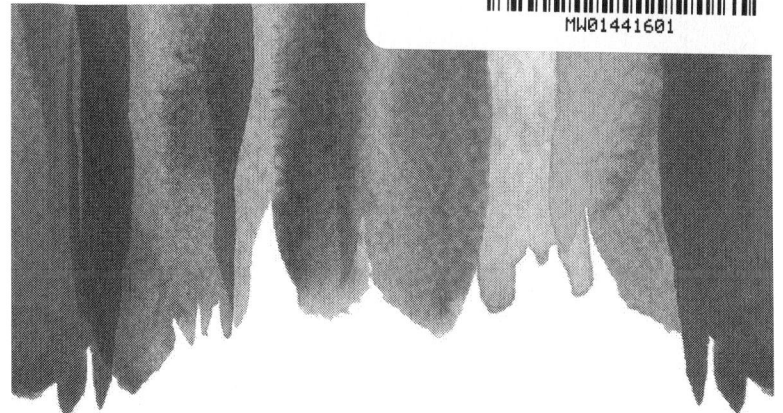

Your Baby

GIRL LIKES GIRLS

ALEX + ALEX

Copyright© 2023 by Alex + Alex Universe

All rights reserved.
Published in the United States
An imprint of Alex + Alex Universe

Alex + Alex Universe books are available via Amazon

Connect with Alex + Alex:

@AlexAndAlexUniverse

@YourBabyGirlLikesGirls

AlexAndAlexUniverse.com

First Edition

*To parents who love their children for who they are.
Who seek understanding with love.
Who are curious enough to evolve.*

CONTENTS

PROLOGUE   7

OUR LOVE STORY   9

ONE: DIPPING YOUR TOES IN   12
Sexuality Is Not a Choice
Sexuality vs. Gender
Coming Out to Herself, Your Daughter's Journey

ALEX RITTER'S STORY   20

ALEX KENWORTHY'S STORY   26

TWO: INITIAL STAGES   30
Your Daughter Hasn't Come Out, Yet
Your Daughter Just Came Out To You
Whoops, I Think I Messed It Up

MADISON'S STORY   42

THREE: PROCESSING — 46
Healthy Outlet: Therapy
Healthy Outlet: Allies
Healthy Outlet: Curiosity
Healthy Outlet: Self-Care

AMARA'S STORY — 52

FOUR: RESETTING EXPECTATIONS — 56
Following In Your Footsteps
Dating
Growing A Family

HANNAH'S STORY — 64

FIVE: WHAT'S NEXT
Coming Out to Family
Coming Out To Community
Coming Out At School
Onward…

JAMIE & KAYLA'S STORY — 76

SIX: GROWING TOGETHER & LOVING EACHOTHER — 81
Encouraging Queer Community
Why Pride is Important
Fanning Her Flame
When Your Daughter Starts Dating
Seeking Out Accepting Environments
Life Is Constantly Evolving
Being An Ally

JULIANA'S STORY 88

SEVEN: YOUR DAUGHTER IS UNIQUE 92
Coming Out Later In Life
Non-Binary & Trans Buddies

EPILOGUE: ELLEN'S STORY 97

Acknowledgments 101

Citations 102

About The Authors 105

PROLOGUE

Your baby girl likes girls! She has either told you OR you have an inkling that she wants to but is still trying to find the courage to take this brave step and tell you her truth.

This moment can be scary for parents–you worry that your relationship with your daughter is changing forever. We're here to tell you the good news: It is! If handled with love, compassion, and an open mind, this can be a beautiful process that brings you together and helps her open up to you like never before.

Our goal for this book is to inspire steps toward your daughter built on healthy communication and understanding. This will lay the foundation for a relationship to grow closer over a lifetime.

While the world has come a long way, the spectrum of sexuality is still a new concept for many. We hope our book will affirm your new normal and help you navigate the reality of who your child is and the world she will inhabit.

Your daughter is sharing her most intimate truth; how you take it and what you do with these moments will shape the path ahead. We've constructed these chapters to guide you on the journey of processing emotions, reevaluating expectations, asking questions, addressing stereotypes, seeking personal growth, and setting healthy boundaries through a compassionate lens.

We will use personal anecdotes of real queer women to highlight the human experiences of these concepts.

We are not clinical psychiatrists or PhDs in human sexuality, nor are we parents. We are just two girls who fell in love and want to help families come together during an experience for which there isn't a cultural template and often has been divisive and hurtful. Through difficulties experienced with our parents, we realized that the hurt could have been avoided if someone had given them a primer to bridge the gap between us. So, here we are!

Differences shouldn't create distance. Differences can remind us how special we are to one another and bring us closer to understanding each other.

May this read lead to beautiful memories.

-Alex & Alex

OUR LOVE STORY

Yes, we're both named Alex. This isn't the craziest thing we have in common.

We met on a spring night in our mid-20s at a local gay hotspot in Los Angeles and immediately felt at home. At the time, we didn't understand the irony of that statement. A couple vodka sodas later, we learned that we had grown up on the same street, in the same sleepy suburban hamlet outside Denver, Colorado, and somehow had never met.

As we ran through our life experiences, we realized we had lived parallel lives, so close together, yet never intersecting. We attended rival Christian/Catholic high schools, then left the state to pursue our collegiate dreams (in Texas and California, respectively). We were both in sororities, both struck out on our own to build ambitious careers. We both love country music, rock & roll, and prefer a night of live music and good wine to just about anything else. We're both only children.

Unfortunately, we have one more thing in common: coming out to our families was painful, which has echoed through our relationships with our parents ever since. The tragedy is that it didn't have to be this way.

At the time of writing this book, we have been together for over five years and are about to celebrate our first wedding anniversary. Though we never thought it could live up to the hype, our wedding day was the most incredible day of our lives. We were married in Denver, surrounded by the people who love us the most, who traveled far and wide to be there. The ballroom was packed with over a hundred loved ones and everyone contributed to a serious blowout.

Alex Kenworthy's parents brought their A-game after coming a long way in their journey toward understanding her sexuality (a journey we will touch on in forthcoming chapters). Alex Ritter was walked down the aisle by her maid of honor and danced to *Just The Way You Are* by Billy Joel with her two uncles following Kenworthy's father-daughter dance. There wasn't a dry eye in the house.

The point is: We're living the epic love story we'd grown up thinking was out of reach. We found our other half, our partner in life and love. We found an antidote for the loneliness we felt when taking those first tentative steps out of the closet.

Does our relationship sound like those you've had in your own life? We're hoping it does because the point is that while our gender may be different from yours, our love stories are not.

Our relationship is built of the same kind of love and devotion as a straight relationship, and your daughter will find this too. This story has so much hope, and we can't wait to share it with you.

We also understand that while we'd lived with ourselves our entire lives, growing, questioning, searching, and finally coming to our authentic truths, all this information was new to our parents. We realize that even if you are ultimately happy for your queer daughter and want her to find her most profound happiness, true love, and togetherness, this new information is a seismic shift from what you had initially understood as her truth.

This is why we wrote this book: to be your allies through this process of entering a new relationship with your daughter. We'll take you through the highs, the lows, the questions, the fears, the pride, and the confusion into understanding and joy.

It's going to be a wonderful ride.

ONE: DIPPING YOUR TOES IN

SEXUALITY IS NOT A CHOICE

Do you remember your first crush? How it hit you like a ton of bricks? You didn't go out of your way to choose the size, weight, and composition of those bricks that knocked you into the next stratosphere of adolescence, did you? The same is true for your daughter.

Sexuality cannot be controlled. It is an unalterable aspect of a person's identity. While it can evolve, sexuality is a profound and indisputable part of a person's fundamental self. If you continue to struggle with this notion, that's all right, but you should trust what your daughter is telling you. This is your first step towards loving her by consciously choosing to believe and accept her. Really, what else matters more than that?

How someone loves and receives love, what gives someone butterflies, what makes them feel electric and alive with another person, is not a choice. It is a chemical expression of their humanity and connection to another person.

While society generally accepts this concept, that hasn't always been the case. You may have been raised in a culture or during a time when the exact opposite of this notion was communicated to you. If this is true, take a moment to be kind to yourself because this was not your fault. Even our ancestors (and some people today) have had to forgive themselves for thinking the Earth was flat. Just like them, take a moment to absorb that you'll need to change these notions you were taught to believe. We're here to provide your telescope.

It may take time to shift homosexual desire from the region in your mind connected to shame and shift it to the region associated with love, beauty, and personal identity. Have compassion for yourself. Our subconscious is a powerful organizing machine that sometimes leaves a red sock in the wash, annoyingly contaminating everything around it. This can be a 'fake it till you make it's situation. But as you sit with this idea, think about your daughter. Think about how much you want her to experience romantic love in her life and how this love lives alongside the romantic love you've experienced. Keeping the focus on your daughter and her happiness, this will feel more and more like the truth.

And even after all this, if you still think sexuality is a choice because she could ultimately choose not to date women, ask yourself: Is asking your daughter to choose loneliness really a life at all? Do you think she can share her gifts with the world if she is closing off the most fundamental human expression there is? Think of what a shame it would be for our world to miss out on her light if she isn't allowed to shine.

We're human beings. We're meant to connect. We'll skip to the end of this existential crisis, so spoiler alert: The meaning of life is love.

SEXUALITY VS. GENDER

One of the barriers to understanding your daughter's queer identity can be the different terminology you didn't grow up with or isn't discussed in your cultural spheres.

You may be thinking, *"why do I need to know this?"* Well, we'll tell you! Beyond educating yourself on the human condition, understanding these concepts will open your mind to seeing which aspects of identity are naturally human, and which have been constructed by society. There is a difference, and understanding this difference will help you understand your daughter, and others around you, in a more complete way.

If a scary bubble of disagreement is expanding in your chest, chill. We'll reiterate:

Have compassion for yourself. It may take time to unravel everything that has been sewn into your mind by previous generations. But as you sit with this idea, think about your child. Think about how much you've loved her since she was born. In keeping your focus on her, your confusion will yield to love. Just like your salad spinner, you'll realize that these old ideas belong at the estate sale.

Below is a primer on terms and concepts that will help you navigate this process.

Settle in, class. This will be on the test.

GAY GLOSSARY:

LGBTQIA+: Stands for Lesbian, Gay, Bisexual, Transgender, Queer/Questioning, Intersex, and Asexual, and the + is inclusive of other orientations and identities that are not considered strictly straight. Easy

Queer vs. **Lesbian** vs. **Bisexual** vs. **Pansexual**

- **Queer:** An inclusive umbrella term used to describe anyone who has feelings or attractions that are not straight, and it is a positive to describe girls who like girls. Queer used to be a pejorative, but our community is reclaiming it as one of pride. Take that, bullies!

- **Lesbian:** We're throwing you a softball here. You know this one. A lesbian is a woman who is attracted to other women.

- **Bisexual:** Someone who is attracted to both people of the same gender and other genders.

- **Pansexual:** Someone who is attracted to a person <u>regardless</u> of their gender.

Sexuality as a spectrum: Refers to the concept of the 'Kinsey Scale,' which posits that a human being falls on a scale of human sexual attraction from zero to six. Boy, was this an instructive tool when we were first coming out. It brought clarity to everything we experienced. On the scale, being a zero refers to 100% heterosexual attraction, and six refers to 100% homosexual attraction. Most of humanity falls somewhere within this spectrum. Asexuals, who do not experience sexual attraction, do not fall on this scale.

Sexuality vs. Gender Identity
- **Sexual Orientation** is an inherent emotional, romantic, or sexual attraction to other people. An individual's sexual orientation is independent of their gender identity. Gender is a construct, people! This leads us to...

- **Gender Identity** is one's innermost concept of self as male, female, a blend of both, or neither. It is how individuals perceive themselves and what they call themselves. One's gender identity can be different from the sex assigned at birth. This is where an individual's pronouns come into play.

- *Side note*: This is a complex conversation on its own and not the express focus of this book. So if your child is also discussing their gender identity with you we highly suggest you give them a huge hug and also seek out additional resources. The Human Rights Campaign website is a great place to start!

- **Transgender:** Transgender is an umbrella term for people whose gender identity is different from their sex assigned at birth.

- **Cisgender**: All this means is someone who doesn't identify as transgender because their gender identity aligns with the sex they were assigned at birth. As the word 'straight' applies to people who aren't queer, so cisgender (or cis) applies to all people who don't identify as trans. Bet you didn't think you'd find yourself on this list!

- **Non-binary/Gender Non-conforming**: Describes a person who does not identify exclusively as a man or a woman. Non-binary people may identify as being both a man and a woman, somewhere in between, or falling completely outside these categories.

- **Pronouns:** Notice how in the previous paragraphs I used inclusive pronouns like 'they' and 'them'. It didn't feel weird, right? Think about that. If your child comes to you discussing their gender identity, think about how language is just our limited way of communicating who we are with each other, and that your language can evolve to represent your child more clearly.
    - If someone informs you of or corrects you on their pronouns, do your best to adjust and respect what that person wants to be called.

Internalized Homophobia: This refers to the homophobia that people on the LGBTQIA+ spectrum was raised with by society that we're still trying to shed to accept ourselves and others in our community. Society ingrains cruel and judgmental messages towards LGBTQIA+ people. We're trying to undergo the same deprogramming as everyone else.

Pride: While Pride is usually a vibrant, glitter-fueled celebration happening in your city in the month of June, it's far more than that. Pride has a deeper meaning of self-affirmation, dignity, equality, and increased visibility of the LGBTQIA+ community as a social group.

Pride is the opposite of shame and stigma. It is a celebration of our community shedding those archaic societal judgments and living authentically. Showing up at a Pride event as a newly out person feels like doing cartwheels and backflips while eating fun-fetti cupcakes all at the same time. We give you permission to be jealous, Pride is awesome.

'Coming Out': A phrase that describes an LGBTQIA+ person first acknowledging, accepting, and appreciating their sexual orientation or gender identity and the process of sharing that with others.

Allies: Last but certainly not least! Allies are those wonderful people who may not fall on the LGBTQIA+ spectrum but actively support the community. In reading this book, you are taking a solid step toward becoming an ally :) Look at you go! You're doing great.

There are additional identities, orientations and concepts that make up the LQBTQIA+ community and then some! We're like the universe, we're constantly expanding. We encourage you to do your research if you have deeper, more nuanced questions.

Now that we've covered the basics let's dive into your relationship with your child! Since the focus of this book and our personal experiences is based on being cisgender women who are attracted to women, we will be using feminine pronouns to describe our experiences. Once again, if your child is discussing their gender identity with you, we want you to scoop them a giant hot fudge sundae and tell your little trans or non-binary bebes that you love them! Then if you get a brain freeze, you should seek out more qualified sources on this topic than two cisgender lesbians.

PS, that was the test! If you understood the terms in this paragraph, you're passing with flying (rainbow) colors!

COMING OUT TO HERSELF: YOUR DAUGHTER'S JOURNEY

Now you're thinking we're full of it, right? The idea that your daughter had to come out of the closet to herself *first* in order to be able to come out to you?

Well, buckle up, Martha.

When we were growing up in ye olde mid-2000s, it was sold to us that you absolutely knew if you were gay since you were a child. We're going to rebuke this popular myth. Not all queer people always knew that they were gay. While many queer people have been aware of their gayness since they were small children, it's not true for everyone.

But wait... aren't we contradicting ourselves, you ask? If we didn't know we were gay, then wasn't it a choice? *Wasn't it??*

Calm down, Gary. We'll get there.

Most of our close queer friends didn't realize the call was coming from inside the house, either. It's a typical joke amongst our community to share stories of that moment when the vertigo hit, and you went, "Holy shit, I'm gay."

For most of us, it took this long because there was very little representation of queer girls living everyday lives. If you didn't stick around Grey's Anatomy long enough to get to the Callie and Arizona relationship, you were shit outta luck.

However, rather than just asking you to take our word for it, we'll tell you, our story.

ALEX RITTER'S STORY

Personally, I must've googled "How do I know if I'm gay?" about a thousand times in my late teens and early 20s. You may ask why I didn't let myself just admit, "Honey, your gay!"

Well, before I knew I was gay, I knew I wasn't supposed to be.

Not only did I grow up in a faith that was against it, there was no one around me that was publicly out. Best case scenario, to come out would've destined me to a life of loneliness. I'd watch my peers obsess over boys and cry over breakups and I'd feel so apart from them. When the idea of being gay would bubble up as the explanation, I would shove it away and tell myself that "I just hadn't been in love yet."

After pretzeling myself into this explanation, I'd have a cooling-off period... but it wouldn't last long. Something else would trigger my suspicion that I was gay.

I'd obsess again; I'd pretzel harder. I convinced myself I didn't have feelings for my beautiful friend or the fiery senior girl in my trig class. I admired them. They were role models. I'd think, "This is how boys feel about Tom Brady, right?" I'd tell myself that girls are just more emotionally connected to their friends, not acknowledging that this feeling was pure and basic longing—a crush.

Nearly every day I would weigh the imaginary scales in my mind with each emotion I felt or reaction I had. Blushing was a common one. So was that "love at first sight" feeling. Thinking back now, the idea that I "admired" a girl before I even spoke to her is the gayest.

In college, I'd get drunk to feel attracted to boys, to match the feelings they felt without trying. When guys chased me down, I'd convince myself that I really did like some of them as people. Maybe they could save me from loneliness. I'd find them sweet and objectively good-looking; sometimes I'd let the positive feelings from their attention masquerade as love and attraction. I'd ache to be chosen, to have someone who understood me. It was an adequate substitute for a while.

Living in this double think for years was exhausting. And it hurt. I'd cry all the time without knowing why. The feelings about girls that flooded out of me were getting harder to tamp down.

As a last-ditch effort, I found a guy to like. The meet-cute was perfect. At one of my best friend's weddings, he was a groomsman, and I was a bridesmaid. Then, when the sadness hit, he accepted me; he had his own demons he was trying to hide. He was as sad as I was. This kindred sadness triggered something for him in my heart. He was a handsome, kind Marine pilot. What girl wouldn't say yes to that? I enjoyed spending time with him, the cross-country flights, and making out in a helicopter. It was exciting, and again, excitement can almost feel like love.

To connect in sadness was the only familiar connection I'd ever had, so for a while this relationship felt right. Then, when he disappeared from my life, I completely fell apart. I knew that what I had with him wasn't the real thing, but I knew that it was as close as I'd ever get with a man. That scared me, and this realization caused the deepest defenses in my core to melt down. I was like an open reactor, spewing radiation into my life. Then, one day I got tired. I gave up fighting and let the truth flood in.

I have the best friends in the universe. I came out to them, and they loved me with the fiercest love I've ever felt. They gave me the strength to go out into the world as my authentic self. They didn't need me to explain the past or the Marine. They accepted my truth as if I was telling them the sky was blue. I was the opposite of lonely, I was loved.

I stepped out of the closet and ventured into gay spaces. When I met my first out lesbian who I would describe as "my type," my longing was so intense I could've thrown up. She kissed me on the cheek. Electricity ran through every inch of my body. A light went on in a corner of my heart that had been dark my whole life.

"Holy shit, I'm gay."

I realized that these feelings were what the rest of the human race has been feeling this whole time. I finally understood those girls in high school who fretted about when the boy would call. I understood the sappy "love you to the moon and back" social media posts. I could imagine relationships that weren't knit together by sadness. It all felt like someone proved to me that Santa Claus was real.

Flash forward to years later, I had that "love at first sight" feeling again. She was a gorgeous, witty bombshell and she swept me away. I fell so hard and so fast that it felt like the properties of gravity recalibrated just to me. About a year ago, she became my wife. I feel full of shit even saying this, but every day is passionate and joyful and full of laughter. Our love is everything.

Sometimes I think back to that sad girl I used to be. I have so much empathy for her now. It's hard to accept the truth.

Without that journey, I wouldn't be able to appreciate how wonderful life is. Now, I get to be happy.

Most of the time now, I wake up forgetting about the fact that I'm gay. I'm too busy living my life and looking forward to the future.

But every once in a while, it hits me, and I can't help but smile.

"Holy shit... I'm gay."

How wonderful is that?

However, there is another side to this story. Alongside my coming out journey, there is also the story of my family.

I waited as long as I could to come out to my parents because I knew they held negative beliefs about the gay community. I have a queer Aunt (my mom's sister), so I knew how she felt about her sexuality. However, I still had a glimmer of hope. I had handfuls of friends tell me how their religious parents surprised them by loving them when they came out, fronting the message that God is love and that they were loved. Or how alternatively, if their parents didn't take it well at first, they have since come around to be more loving and accepting than my friends ever thought possible.

Unfortunately, that is not my family's story. My parents did not accept it and that has not changed. Shame, disgust, and sin dominated the conversation and continued in each ensuing interaction. For years I didn't have a conversation with my mom without her crying. My dad told me that this was God calling me to the single life. His stance holds strong that this isn't what a life of honor and integrity looks like, that the noble choice would be to sacrifice my happiness in order to do what is "right."

As mentioned, I am an only child. It became two against one. Their focus was on how I could do this to them. What did they do to deserve this? They said it was like losing a child, which they knew all about having already lost two children within days of their birth due to medical complications.

The distance between us grew. They retreated further into Catholic doctrine and away from me. They texted paragraphs of Bible verses and indignation every time I'd post a picture of Alex and me on social media with a demand to take it down. They stopped seeing some of their closest friends because they were ashamed. My therapist explained that caring so much about what other people think comes from their failure to accept that <u>this is reality</u>. If no one ever knew about me being gay it would go away, it wouldn't be real.

But it is real. I am real. My love is real.

When Alex and I became serious, they tolerated her presence at dinners as much as they could, but they couldn't hide their malcontent. When Alex and I got engaged, they conveyed they would not be present or support our wedding. They believed it was not a real marriage in the eyes of God, that I was committing to a life of sin, and their faith called them to not support me on that day. We've had very limited contact since then, emails to update on health, and the administrative situations that come from being a legal family.

Alex Kenworthy's mom, Ellen, bought my wedding dress. My best friend's mother, Darcy, presented me with a family heirloom to wear, "something borrowed," that she'd worn on her wedding day. My uncles Joe and Chris danced with me during the "father/daughter" dance. My maid of honor walked me down the aisle.

This severing from my immediate family is a deep wound that never heals, no matter how much peace I make with reality. I've embarked on a healing journey to find ways to love myself in place of where my parental love should be. It's affected how secure I feel in relationships. Alex lovingly understands my separation anxiety and overall general anxiety that the ground can drop out from under me at any minute, or that I am disposable to those in my life. For a long time, I had nightmares every night about being separated from Alex or being trapped in rooms with my parents as they tried to erase me. I still have them at least once a week.

It's real trauma. I've learned to cope. I'd change it if I could. Acceptance is understanding that I can't change other people, their choices, or the past.

It is a sad story; I tell it because I want you and your daughter's story to be different. I'd like you to avoid similar trauma if you can. I believe that it doesn't have to be this hard. I believe that love wins.

ALEX KENWORTHY'S STORY

Your daughter's story is as unique as she is. Though we grew up on the same street, our experiences were different.

> Coming out to myself has been a thirty-two-year effort, kind of like how Uncle Bob has been "on a diet" since 1998 but hasn't lost a pound. That's me, I'm Bob. Bear with me.
>
> For context, I grew up a tomboy. If you saw a picture of me at seven years old, it's painfully shocking that my parents didn't know all along. I played hockey, wore JNCO jeans, and got a Jonathan Taylor Thomas haircut. Some would say I was FLAMING and that someone is ME. If nature was allowed to take its course, I would've been "out" as early as second grade.
>
> I was a very intuitive child; my guess is being closeted and hyper-aware of expectations and perceptions are connected. The human brain will do what it needs to in order to survive and thrive in the world, and that is my story.
>
> By middle school, I adapted. Stylistically, I became as straight as a five-dollar footlong. I had plenty of friends, I was outgoing and good at sports. I was popular, social, and bold. By high school, I had interest from boys. I dated older and generally someone who had interest from other girls. Attention and attraction were interchangeable at the time. I couldn't differentiate between them. I honestly thought I liked the boys I dated.
>
> In college, I continued to disassociate from my feelings by fitting in. I rushed a sorority and had the blond hair, high fashion, in-crowd down. I had a multi-year relationship with a man. I have

regrets because I broke some truly wonderful hearts by not understanding why I didn't love them back the way they loved me.

Here's the kicker... throughout this time, I was having side relationships with women. We never called it what it was, we didn't acknowledge it out loud. I never looked it in the eye. It's like I blacked out all those instances until I was in my mid-20s. I compartmentalized so deeply that I never thought I was cheating, and I never considered that it meant I was gay. It sounds crazy, but gay didn't exist in my life.

It was easy to watch other girls have close female friendships and not understand how I was different, so I would categorize my relationships into that bucket. Not facing my feelings made my emotions polarizing. It became hard for me and those closest to me to understand why I was agitated or completely shut down at times.

My senior year of college I got into a program in New York City that moved me out of Waco, Texas for my final semester. I had just broken up with a boyfriend of two years and had a falling out with a best friend who was more than that for me. It was the first time I acknowledged that she broke my heart, which felt significantly more excruciating than the multiyear boyfriend I broke up with.

During this time, I got on dating apps and set my profile to women. Cue the Taylor Swift "Welcome to New York" anthem (yasss). It was an awakening. I couldn't pretend or lie to myself any longer. The double life was not sustainable. I knew who I was and was abundantly aware that it would blow up my life. Seventeen years of Christian schooling didn't set me up with an understanding community.

I came out to my family and friends back home. It wasn't a joyous experience and became the domino that moved my life to the west coast to this day. I was gutted. I lost every straight male friend I had, most of whom were best friends of more than seven years. I didn't realize their consistency came from wanting more than friendship. It was a painful betrayal and shredded the confidence I'd carried my entire life. I lost everything. I felt more me than ever before, while simultaneously needing to rebuild my identity.

These experiences led to years of anxiety and internalized homophobia. I struggled to embrace this part of myself and hid it from the outside world. This is ironic given that I blew up my life to own who I was. I kicked off a career in sales. I now run a sales team on the West Coast, but into my 20s I kept my private life private to the people I worked with. I worried if I didn't dress, look, sound, and act a certain way that it would alter the trajectory of my career. It's hard to say if I was wrong, it worked.

I often wonder what fulfillment and accomplishments could have come my way if I hadn't been overanalyzing every little thing I said or did for years of my life. I resented peers who I knew would never be judged for who they were, who walk through the world lightly. When you lose people at a rapid rate, when love becomes clearly conditional, it changes how you walk through life.

Please, have grace for the weight your daughter is carrying–it can be crushing.

Then I met Alex, and hiding the most beautiful part of my world was no longer an option. Since I'd professionally established myself, I ripped off the band-aid. Then the craziest thing happened: my coworkers, superiors, and those in my world showered me with love and support. The world I spent five years building was drastically different from where I grew up and had room in its heart for a flaming Texas sorority lesbian to thrive.

I hope your takeaway from our stories is that coming out takes as long as it takes, there's no rushing it. Everyone is ready at their own pace.

TWO: INITIAL STAGES

YOUR DAUGHTER HASN'T COME OUT...
BUT YOU THINK SHE MIGHT

As a parent, you've known your daughter her entire life. If she has also chosen a Jonathan Taylor Thomas haircut, you may have an inkling that she plays for a different team than her peers. Maybe you're curious about a lack of interest in boys, or an over-interest that feels inauthentic like she's compensating for something. If it's the latter, this doesn't mean her sexuality isn't already defined, but that she is investigating the truth of it in her life. The point is, you think you might know something, but since she hasn't told you it's TBD.

Here comes the hard part. At this point in time, the best thing you can do is **wait for her to come to you**. Frustrating, I know. The first advice we're giving you is to do nothing! We'll tell you why.

Telling her you know something about her that she is still trying to figure out for herself could push her further into the closet. Before she truly embraces herself, the fear can be overwhelming, and having other people tell you that they know you better than you know yourself is damaging to your self-esteem. Being *ready* to come out is important, so it's best to give her the space she needs to get comfortable with her identity before sharing it with you.

Cue a relevant anecdote from Alex Ritter. That's right, more stories!

When I was finally ready to come out, one of the first people I told was my cousin, Kristin. I was so nervous, but a knowing smile spread across her face when the words came out of my mouth. She told me that almost a year prior, after a late night on the town, I had come out to her but... had forgotten by the following day (don't worry, darlings, I was over 21). Kristin had known since that night, but she waited for me to be ready to share my truth with her. I can't tell you how much love she showed me in waiting. When I finally came out (again) she'd saved all her excitement for that moment and showered me with love. Our bond has only strengthened since.

During this time of waiting, something positive you can do is foster an open-minded and loving relationship. Remind your daughter that you love her for who she is and that nothing could cause you to love her less.

You can also make it clear that you have a progressive point of view when it comes to the natural differences between human beings. Remind her that it doesn't matter what someone looks like, who they date, or how they fit into social groups or gender norms–that's not what gives them value as a person. A person is most valuable when they are being their authentic self. Our differences make the human race lush and interesting.

Now, if you think your daughter might be a target of bullying, this is another matter. Bullies suck, and unfortunately, they can exist anywhere. If you believe your daughter is being bullied, we encourage you to seek resources in your area to navigate this situation. Below is a list of places to start...

-**The Trevor Project:** TheTrevorProject.org/resources

-**The Gay, Lesbian, Straight Education Society:** Glsen.org

-**StopBullying.gov**/bullying/lqbtq

YOUR DAUGHTER JUST CAME OUT TO YOU

It happened. She told you. Elvis has left the building. She may have said something like...

"I like girls," "I'm queer," "I'm not straight," "I'm a lesbian," or "I'm gay."

There are a million ways she could have told you, but the point is: she told you. Turn down the game, George, and let it soak in. She likes girls!

Wow! This is a huge moment, no matter how much she may have downplayed it. She has chosen to show you her truest self. I hope you can feel our glitter-tossing fist pump from here. This is a beautiful time for your relationship and a memory to cherish.

Your brain may be spinning with questions about the rainbow confetti gram she just dropped in your lap. But here is the first, most important thing to keep in mind, no matter how old your daughter is. We said it before, now this time with a megaphone...

Trust her.

Trust that she knows herself better than anyone else does. This might be hard, as you've known her before she could walk or talk or ask herself questions of identity. Your love for her started it all. What you know of her has been built up over years, decades even, and what she's telling you could seem incongruent with what you've known her to be. However, what you should know is that before this moment, she has spent countless hours soul-searching. She has been gradually uncovering the truth at the center of her soul, and it isn't something she's flippantly deciding to try out. It isn't a phase, Lorraine!

Even if her feelings have been subconscious for years, she's been looking at the world, seeing where she fits, her similarities, her differences, and spending time with her own deep feelings in order to understand them. Even if she blurts it out casually, or if you stumble upon it while doing her laundry, it's been simmering below the surface, and she's been interrogating it for longer than you realize.

So, this isn't a moment for you to start this process over at square one.

Clutch your pearls, Cindy, there's no stopping this train.

Try to avoid saying things like:

> *"Are you sure you're not confusing attraction with friendship?"*

> *"We all have feelings for our close friends; this doesn't mean you are attracted to women."*

> *"We all have girl crushes; I have one on Jessica Alba."*

> *"You won't really know who you are until you're older."*

> "Why didn't you tell us sooner? We could have talked it through."
>
> "Sometimes girls kiss girls; that doesn't mean you're queer."

While you may think you're being helpful, these comments are a big bummer. Bummers are what we're trying to avoid. These phrases invalidate your daughter's judgment of herself and tell her that other people, specifically her elders, know her better than she knows herself. Flashback to your own personal journey (oh, the leg warmers) and give her the same respect you gave yourself to figure it out. Even if, as a parent, you understand how long it's taken you to discover yourself, it is not your job to dictate her journey to her.

This a billboard moment. The billboard is telling you to respect this boundary as a parent. This is a moment to absorb your daughter's truth instead of trying to place yourself in her shoes and impart your life's journey onto her.

As this moment evolves, you may be unsure of what to say or how to react ("And what do I do with my hands!") but remember this: **your North Star is compassion.** Lead with compassion, and it will steer you well.

What does compassion look and sound like?

WHAT TO SAY:

Tell her you love her. It's so simple, there's no need to reinvent the wheel. In this instance that is what she is worried may change. She is worried that revealing her most vulnerable self could cause you to love her less or change the way you see her in some way, so reassure her that this has not happened.

Other great options include: ***"I love you just the way you are"*** or ***"Nothing could ever change my love for you."*** Embrace the cheese, people! This is your moment for feelings charcuterie.

Tell her you're honored that she's sharing her truth with you. She probably hasn't come out to many people yet, so being one of the first to know, and telling her that you cherish that honor, will build her self-worth. Self-worth is the armor she needs to take her truth into the world.

Tell her that this honesty makes you happy because her happiness is important to you! As your daughter, seeing her live joyfully and authentically is all a parent could want, right? That smile makes your world go round. Communicate this to her!

Ask her how you can support her. The subsequent phases of her journey can involve telling other family members, friends, or the community. It can get exhausting. Ask her how you can support her during this process, and be ready with whatever double-fudge, salted-caramel concoction takes the edge off. Don't forget the rainbow sprinkles, obviously.

All I want is for you to be happy. Again, the basics are rad. Isn't this the most essential thing you could want for your daughter? Sometimes the simplest messages get lost in the moment, so even though you might think it goes without saying, say it! It will mean the world to her. Your daughter wants to know that being herself doesn't cause you pain. She won't be able to be happy and love herself if she knows that it does. So if you are feeling complex emotions, return to this simple principle.

Our other advice is to keep this moment about this moment.

We know you have so many questions. *What about that boy you dated? Have you ever kissed a girl? Who all have you told?* **This is not the time to address these questions, Pamela!**

This is a moment to *listen* to what she is ready to tell you. She probably has a whole Ted Talk ready, so locate your nearest comfy chair and sit your ass down. Let this moment connect you with your child as a growing person and in this shared experience of humanity. Embrace this moment with the same love you have had for her since the day she was born, instead of getting bogged down in what you've observed of her life up until this point.

Responding by listening will go a long way in making your child feel secure in your relationship and in your home. The more assured she feels of your allyship, the closer your relationship will be.

Okay, now let's get to your feelings, concerns, fears, and questions. Don't beat yourself up for having these, you are human, and we live in a complex culture rife with hurtful stereotypes and short on positive models. You're probably thinking about your own upbringing, what you were told about "being gay," what it means, and the images in the media that represented this identity to you.

Here's the hard part, but we're going to tell it to you straight (look at us with the puns) because we want the best for your relationship with your daughter. **It is not your daughter's job to be your therapist.** She has done her job, which is being honest with you, living her life and being herself. Now, she's got pep rallies or drag races or whatever she likes to get back to. Any other tidbits, details, explanations, anecdotes or ah-ha moments are hers to share with you and are not to be extracted via interrogation. This is the second instance of maintaining **healthy boundaries.** That is your anthem.

Sing it with us, JLo! Let's get loud! Too much? Get used to it. The queers love going over the top… and JLo.

Another point: It's also not your daughter's job to explain the tapestry of human sexuality to you unless she volunteers to. Meaning, **she is not your teacher.** If you have questions, you're going to have to do some self-educating. Please do. Nothing is more awkward than explaining the spectrum of sexuality to your parents. Well, maybe watching Black Swan in theaters together… be lucky you missed out on that.

If you have fears or concerns, that's normal! We will help you through this process in later chapters. Don't worry, we weren't going to leave you hanging.

Below is a list of phrases to avoid to keep y'all smooth sailing.

NO-NO PHRASES:

"How do you know you're queer/gay/bi/pan?"

By now you already get it, but we'll say it again for posterity: The only real answer to this question is something that she's already told you by coming out: she likes girls.

"This isn't a good time."

Let's say she blurts out her truth right before you leave for work or before Mimaw comes to visit. Keep perspective; whatever else is going on in the roller coaster of life pales in comparison to this moment. Give this moment the respect it deserves, and if it needs to be a conversation that you finish at another time, tell her that you can't wait to give this conversation the space it needs.

"You're not allowed to tell anyone."

Oof, there's no sugar-coating it. This one is a doozy we both heard from our parents and still stings. As your child, it's hurtful for her to hear that her parents are so ashamed of her that she has to keep herself a secret from your bridge group, softball league, and the PTA. Here's the deal: whether it's your friends, church, coworkers, grandparents, or the internet, it is her choice whom to tell and when. All you should do is support her in that choice.

"What will other people think?"

This is more of a sub-point to the above, but no harm in elaborating. I'm sure you're nervous about how her old-school grandfather is going to feel about this, but this is not the moment to discuss it. Your worries are not her responsibility to carry. Saying this tells her that what other people think is more important than her worth as a person, and this is damaging to the self-esteem she will need when interacting with people who will have opinions about her.

"How do you know you're queer if you haven't had sex with a man?"

First, this isn't about men. Men are the furthest thing from your daughter's mind during this conversation. Second, yeesh. Did you like your parents interrogating you about your sex life, Phil? Real talk: Over-asking or oversharing about sex in a way that makes your daughter so uncomfortable she wants to evaporate is crossing a boundary. Asking her about boyfriends she's had in the past is irrelevant at this point. If a lousy ex-boyfriend or two could turn someone gay, then there would be no straight women left.

Starting off on this respectful foot will take you a long way. If she wants to add anything on the topic, or if she wants to explain her journey through these experiences with you, she will volunteer to. If she does, we recommend having a nice bottle of tequila nearby. You are human. However, let her know that this discussion, or these explanations, aren't required for you to believe and trust her.

"Is my kid going to be a whore?"

Okay, Cheryl. We'll entertain this archaic question because I'm sure it's floating around your knitting circle, and someone needs to answer it for you. Time to put on your big girl panties for some talk about sex: If your daughter hasn't had a sex life yet, she probably will now that she knows what she wants. It isn't her queerness causing her to have sex, it's knowing who she likes, just like all straight people. However many sexual partners your child has, that is really her business, so don't pry into that Pandora's box and don't judge her for living her life.

"Is sex between two women actually sex?"

Oh, Cheryl, we meet again. Since most of us were raised to believe that it isn't sex unless there is a penis in the mix, we're going to blow your mind here with a new definition. Nowadays, we understand sex to include all intimate contact between two partners involving fingers, mouths, and genitals. Ask yourself this philosophical thought experiment: "If a tree in the forest orgasms a thousand times, is it still a virgin?" This answer should be obvious... no. That tree has had sex, even if it hasn't been penetrated by a penis.

"Our religion forbids this."

If you are using religion to shame your daughter out of being herself, STOP. If you come from a faith background, this topic is important, but should not be used as a weapon against her or as righteous reasoning for her to change. Unless she brings it up in her coming out moment, it's crucial to establish how much you love her and how strong your relationship is before bringing the complexities of faith and practicing religion into the conversation.

The important thing at this time is to keep the focus on your daughter, this moment, and your love for her. Do not bring the rest of the world and situations you can't control into this sacred space.

There are also additional resources beyond what is listed here. We highly recommend seeking out a PFLAG (Parents and Friends of Lesbians and Gays) group in your area, especially if your child is an adolescent. This group is a safe space and a lifeline for *your* journey alongside your daughter's.

WHOOPS, I THINK I MESSED IT UP

If, when your daughter came out, you said a few of these 'Phrases to Avoid' before you found this book...

You're totally screwed!

Just kidding. Take a breath.

If something you said triggered a fight or upset emotions, take some space to cool off. There's nothing you can do about the past. All you can do is...

Forgive yourself.

There will be opportunities to return to a loving place after this moment. If you were wrong, **tell her so** and rectify the situation. It is vital that you take ownership of the words and emotions you communicate to her instead of blaming them on stress or expecting her to discard hurtful things that were said. Apologize and ask her if you can understand further. It will go a long way toward strengthening your bond. Good thing you have that salted-caramel pint ready.

Now, let's air the sad out. Time for some good news! Now that you've moved on from this heightened moment, there are several positive steps you can take that will cultivate a loving relationship.

We encourage you to spend time with your daughter doing fun things. Too many serious conversations can make your relationship feel heavy. We can only talk about being queer so much. It really isn't that complex! The last thing you want is your relationship to feel like a chore. If you and your daughter aren't used to doing activities together, there's no better time to start. Having a joint hobby can be bonding, plus if you kick her butt at mini golf, you have bragging rights for life. It's a win-win.

MADISON'S STORY

Our friend Madison is from a big Italian family on the East Coast. Below is her story...

"I'm one of five sisters, right in the middle. My parents lived two hours from New York City, but we didn't go often. I grew up in a town where everybody knows everybody."

"Where I grew up, being [LGBTQ+] wasn't really discussed. The only gay person I knew was my uncle on my dad's side, who lived in California at the time. I didn't know that anybody cared."

"Growing up, my mom was good about letting us express ourselves. If I wanted to dress like a Tomboy she was all, "that's fine if you want to wear that. You're expressing yourself. You're figuring yourself out." My parents weren't uptight about what the community at large thought.

"I realized I liked girls freshman year of high school. I went to a public high school in a city. I had a friend whose sister was bisexual and when my friend explained what that meant, I was like, "Oh!" I hadn't known that that was an option. When I looked back, this made sense for me. There were girls that I gravitated towards, or who made me feel anxious. People would ask me, "Why are you being so weird about this girl?" I realized I was being weird because I liked her."

"I told my high school friends that I was bi, and a couple others were like "me too!" So that was high school. Nobody cared, everyone was fine with it. I knew I wasn't doing anything wrong, so if you thought it was wrong, I felt like, "That's on you.""

"In my experience, people's level of acceptance was more about geography than it was about religion or anything else. With city schools you have more of an open mindset. I'd even gone to a Catholic school in the city. There were a bunch of gay people there. Nobody cared."

"Then I transferred to a public high school in a smaller town. They had small mindsets. There were no gay people there. So, when I was this little Tomboy going around and saying, "I'm gay, I have a girlfriend," I was the only one doing that. My girlfriend at the time went to another school, but there were two other girls at this school who had been dating for a long time and weren't telling anyone. I asked them, "Why is it a secret? Who cares?" But the parents at this school cared. This was the only school I ever went to where the parents had aggressive opinions."

"My sister who was three years older knew I'd liked girls since I was a freshman. She didn't have an opinion about it. None of my sisters did. My youngest sister was thirteen when I came out to her [years later]. She also didn't care. She's a generation younger than me and they couldn't care less about people being queer."

"I don't know how my parents didn't know sooner. I had a feeling that my mom would have a negative reaction to it, so I avoided telling her for a long time. The weird thing was that I knew that they knew I was lying. I wish they would've come towards me and said that it would be okay [to come out]."

"I'd started dating a serious girlfriend (let's call her Katie), when I was twenty-four. My mom asked if she was my girlfriend. She had been piecing it together. But at the time, my younger sister was about to leave for college. I knew that if I said "yes," my mom would have her fit about it, so I said "no." I didn't want to take the shine away from my sister who needed my parents' attention more."

"Then, months later Katie was at my birthday dinner. My grandfather was asking my younger sister, "Who is this girl Madison keeps bringing around?" My mom interjected and said she knew what was going on, and that Katie was my girlfriend. So then I was like, "Okay, fine. Yes, Katie is my girlfriend.""

"After that night, my mom ignored my calls. Eventually, when she answered the phone, she said, "I don't accept this." My response was that she needed to calm down because it's not a big deal."

"My mom has an old-school mindset. Both of my parents were raised Catholic. She has a "this is how things are done," attitude. I think she was hoping that she wouldn't have to confront a new idea about my life, but to this day I don't really know why she had intense feelings about it."

"My mom said, "This is going to destroy your father." I ripped off the band-aid and texted him, "Mom says this is going to destroy you, so I'm sorry if it does, but I want to let you know that Katie is my girlfriend." His response was, "Oh, cool. Does she want to come to Long Island with us tomorrow?" It was as chill as that. He understood that this is about my happiness. My dad doesn't care about anything else."

"After that, my mom ignored me for two weeks, so all my sisters told her, "If you don't talk to Madison, then we don't talk to you. You either have five kids or you have no kids." Family is really important to my mom, so when it came down to her needing to accept me or no one would talk to her, she started to come around."

"For Thanksgiving that year there was a discussion about whether or not there would be a space for Katie. My dad told my mom, "Madison bringing Katie is the same thing as her sisters bringing their boyfriends." She understood that. From then on, she turned a corner and came towards me. Every girlfriend I've ever had, my dad's taken us on a trip together. He's very sweet and thoughtful. My grandpa eventually found out and didn't care. Even my grandma who has dementia asks when my girlfriend is coming over."

"My mom's come a long way. She bought my girlfriend and me a Christmas ornament this year that says "love is love." To me it says that she wants me to know that she supports me and loves me."

"My older sister has kids, so I have a niece and a nephew. We're normalized to them the way my uncle and his boyfriend were normalized to us. It's the easiest thing in the world for them to understand. They send my girlfriend and I valentines in February."

"My girlfriend and I don't really get hassled in public. I've always lived in accepting places. Since I'm femme presenting and usually date girls who are femme presenting, we don't get bothered. If a boy won't leave me alone, I give him a stare that tells him to move along."

"Yeah. I'm just living my life the way everyone else is."

THREE: **PROCESSING**

Now that your daughter has come out and you've had these initial conversations, eventually the realities of life return. You'll move on to figuring out what to eat for dinner, taking the dog to the vet, going to work, school, and if you're anything like us, popping the cork on a nice cab. Cheers, queers, and loved ones!

Now it's important for you to spend time with yourself, processing.

As discussed in the previous section, not burdening your daughter with your processing and/or expecting her to be your therapist is essential to keeping your relationship healthy. However, if you do not take the time to process how you are feeling and seek your own support, your anxieties will ultimately bubble up into your relationship and create a toxic dynamic. This falls under the category of 'bummer' that we're trying to avoid. Nothing is a bigger bummer than you angsting about grandma's reaction or asking about the Bible right before she's about to sink a putt through the windmill on the 9th hole. However, you do need a supportive place to take your deepest questions.

HEALTHY OUTLET: THERAPY

Finding a therapist that specifically specializes in LGBTQIA+ family issues can be a great outlet to seek information, process your emotions, and gain support in navigating your expanding worldview. No matter where in the world you are, there are many fabulous therapists available via Zoom.

Specifically, finding a therapist that you feel understands you as a person is important as well. Picking a therapist that you don't feel like you can be truly honest with, and share the deepest most vulnerable feelings with, is a waste of time. For instance, finding a therapist that not only specializes in LGBTQIA+ issues but also specializes in your religion or culture can make a huge difference.

If you're someone who thinks therapy isn't for you, many people feel that way. Probably many other people in your family. However, I would encourage you to at least try it out. Like a crop top, or the color burgundy. It could suit you and you would've had no idea.

You are entering a brave new world of expanding your horizons to understand your daughter. This can be scary–challenging ingrained patterns always is–but this step towards embracing the unknown could yield surprising results and provide relief from the emotions you've been bottling up.

HEALTHY OUTLET: ALLIES

Nowadays, everyone at least tangentially knows someone who is queer or identifies on the LGBTQIA+ spectrum. If not, I feel bad for the low-vibes township you're living in, but we can work with it. You might not immediately know whom to confide in, but this can be a beautiful time to open up to your friends and community (that belong to you, not your daughter's community) about your relationship with your daughter. If you know someone with a queer child, they could be a tremendous first ally. Like the children's books tell us, you're never too old to make new friends.

Finding someone who's been in your shoes and has a loving relationship with their child could be an excellent outlet you didn't know you needed. One red flag to look for: If this person still feels negatively about their child's queerness, then yikes. This person won't be a healthy relationship and you should try another friendship for solace. Wet blankets don't brighten up anyone's picnic.

I'm going to reiterate something from the previous paragraph: do not choose someone from your child's world to be your confidant. While you can have the best intentions, you want to avoid triangulating, which feels like you are bringing someone else's opinion of your daughter's identity into your relationship with your daughter. You do not want her to think that this person's input is more valid than hers. Triangulation can often feel like an attempt to change your daughter. It isn't cool for her to be at her friend's wedding and have the mother of a friend come up to her and give her two cents about your daughter's sexuality and her relationship with her parents... for example.

Once you find someone you can confide in, or even if you've found a few people, have regular contact with them. Friendship dates! The more you spend time with loving and accepting models for you to emulate, the easier it will be. Also, you will be much happier. The converse is also true: the more time you spend with those who have negative opinions of your daughter's truth, the more their toxic viewpoints will take root in your mind and grow sad judgmental beanstalks.

You might not know at first who is a friendly ally, so as you develop your relationship with this person, trust your gut. If someone gives you judgmental or performative vibes, swipe left.

This can feel like a daunting step. It's normal to feel vulnerable opening up to another person. However, remember your North Star: growing into a compassionate and loving relationship with your daughter. Keeping that in mind should give you some inner strength to take this step.

Once you do, I promise that people will surprise you. You'll be shocked to learn that many people you know are in a similar boat and raising a child in the LGBTQIA+ community. We've seen parents gain lifelong friendships with people they previously saw as acquaintances by bonding over their queer children.

Another avenue of connection, if your child is still in school, are support groups of other parents with LGBTQIA+ children. PFLAG groups (Parents and Friends of Lesbians and Gays) meet regularly and find solidarity in their experience with a safe space to ask questions, express their feelings, concerns, and fears, and find a supportive community that helps them embrace the joy of having a queer child.

HEALTHY OUTLET: CURIOSITY

Society has traditionally had such a blind spot for our community that you'll be surprised how much there is to get curious about! Peek into our tidepool. Getting curious about the LGBTQIA+ community around you will open your worldview and help you understand your daughter's experience.

For instance, did you know that Eleanor Roosevelt, in addition to being a badass political leader, diplomat, and humanitarian, was also a queer woman? Or Sally K. Ride, the first American woman to travel in space? Or playwright, Lorraine Hansberry?

Now that you're caught up on some history, we're going to blow your mind with the sheer number of impressive queer women storming our world today. From global music superstars Lady Gaga and Demi Lovato to soccer phenom Megan Rapinoe, from comediennes Kate McKinnon and Margaret Cho to Poet Laureate Audre Lorde, Emmy-winning writer Lena Waithe and Good Morning America host Robin Roberts. There's Supermodel Cara Delevingne, and actresses Tessa Thompson, Aubrey Plaza, and Sarah Paulson. Oh, and let's not forget NASA astrophysicist, Dr. Jane Rigby!

Curiosity can lead to the realization that this community is just as varied and diverse as the "straight world." You'll see that not all queer women dress the same, act the same, are attracted to the same type, have the same ambitions, opinions, likes, or dislikes. A queer woman is just as likely to be a ballet dancer as she is a mechanic or even both. Now that's the kind of girl I want rewiring my transmission.

The point here is: Let your curiosity show you that your daughter can be anyone and anything she wants to be in this community, and she will belong all the same. Also, there is so much joy in the queer world, pop your heart in for a recharge.

It is human to be cautious or even a little afraid of a community that is different from you and wonder if they are healthy for your daughter. We assume that some of you have chosen to first to step outside of your comfort zone in the safety of your own environment by reading this book. While these feelings are human, I challenge you to look at your daughter, this community and its many unique individuals through a lens of curiosity and respect. Embrace the naturally diverse spectrum of humanity outside of the community. You may just notice your fears melt away, and you'll realize that our differences make humankind beautiful.

HEALTHY OUTLET: SELF CARE

As a parent, it can be difficult to find time to indulge in activities that are just for you. It can feel like everyone else's needs should come first, or that it is selfish to think about yourself. False!

Self-care is as critical as therapy and community outreach because it gives you an opportunity to love yourself and feel your emotions in a productive way. Self-love is important because the more you appreciate yourself for all your uniqueness, the more you will love your daughter for all of hers.

This is also a healthy time to get out of your head and take a break from overthinking all of this. Obsessing is exhausting, just ask your daughter. The more you embrace the rest of your life and other interests, the better your perspective will be. Let yourself take a breath and chill out.

AMARA'S STORY

Our friend Amara is from a Midwestern Black family. She grew up Catholic.

"I'm from the Midwest. The city I grew up in isn't a big city but it also isn't small. There weren't any out gay people there, so it was almost like no one was gay. I knew there were gay people in the world, but I just didn't associate them with my community."

"My parents wanted us to go to Catholic schools. I didn't mind the uniforms or the Catholic part of it, but being gay was considered sinful. I was so dissociated from it that I didn't think I was gay, even though I knew I had feelings for girls."

"I realized I was gay in my early 20s but didn't come out for years. I was out to other gay people, but no one else. No one in my family, at work, or old friends."

"I went to a big state school for college, so I finally started to meet different kinds of people there. My sophomore year, Lady Gaga came out [as bisexual]. I had a crush on her. I started to think that I might be bi. I thought I liked guys still, but I was realizing that I wasn't straight. There was a guy I started dating my junior year, but the one time we were intimate I hated it. I was like, "I can't do this." It made me realize I was probably gay because I didn't like guys at all."

"After college, I moved to Los Angeles. I was out in LA, but not to my family, work life or old friends. I was living two separate lives. I coped by throwing myself into work."

"My parents would ask me if I was dating anyone, they wanted me to meet someone. But after I'd moved to LA, I just shut off. I stopped talking about my personal life altogether. I have two brothers and I was so secretive, even to them. One brother once asked me if I was secretly married. Everyone thought it was super weird for the longest time."

"After years and years, I finally came out to my oldest brother. We're close. He's my backbone. He always knew something was up. We grew up together and did everything together. I'm the epitome of a late bloomer, but having never been in a relationship all that time... It was weird. I was just so shy with my sexuality that it was hard to meet anyone. I knew I needed to come out, and he was the best. With him on my side, I knew he would tell my parents to chill. He's an open-minded guy. And then my other brother was chill too."

"Five months later, out of the blue, my parents asked me if I was gay. I'd already been feeling like I needed to come out to them. I couldn't live this double life anymore. I had just been at a gay bar in LA and was in a picture with a couple of girls. The next day, my mom called and asked me, "Amara, I need to ask you a question: are you gay?" I said yes, and then I started crying."

"Their reaction wasn't that bad. My dad cried a little. My parents are okay, they're just distant. My mom said, "I don't really understand that." It wasn't a long conversation. Afterward, they both texted me separately and said, "We love you." But I still feel the distance. We don't ever talk about it. My life is very gay, but they only want to talk about the aspect of my life that isn't–which is work. I don't talk to them about my friends, who I date, or what I do to have fun. My job is only a part of me. There's so much more to me than that. It gets to a point where we really don't have much to talk about anymore.

They'll ask me what's wrong, but I feel like I can't talk about the things in my life that I'm having feelings about."

"I hate that I don't have that relationship with my parents. I hate that I can't talk to them about something like having a hard time with a friend. I can't talk to them about it because that friend might be gay. I've seen how they are with my brothers and their friends and their lives, there is a difference. That's where I get sad. My parents are so integrated with my brothers' friends. It's hard. It's like 'don't ask, don't tell' at home."

"My dad is more realistic about it. He gets that I want to have a relationship of my own. My mom would rather not think about me having somebody. I'd love to feel comfortable saying, "I want to have a partner" and have them respond that they want me to have that too. I'd like them to say, "We want you to be happy and we can't wait for the time when you bring somebody home." I don't want them living in fear about what's going to happen or what it's going to be like when I do."

"I think where my parents live contributes to their difficulty with it. They're still in the town I grew up in. Their imagination [of what humans can be like] is limited to what they've seen there. I think their root of uncomfortability is more about having a daughter they didn't think would be like this and that I'm so weird. They had an idea of what my life would look like and they have to change that. I think it's less about them thinking that being gay is wrong."

WHAT WOULD YOU SAY TO OTHER PARENTS WHO SIMILARLY DON'T KNOW HOW TO TALK TO THEIR QUEER DAUGHTERS ABOUT THEIR LIVES?

"Ask questions. Ask how they feel and why. I wish my parents asked me more of these kinds of questions. You don't have to ask deep questions about girls and what I like, but just treat me like a human. The only thing different about me is that I like women, I date them and am attracted to them. Other than that, I have the same emotions. Please try to understand that this isn't something I chose, but I am here in this world, and I do want to at least enjoy it like everyone else."

"I want that kind of equality. I really hope they could see me as an equal, as a normal person who wants to be asked questions about who I am with the intent of actually understanding me."

WHAT IS YOUR HOPE FOR THE FUTURE?

"I hope that one day it won't be a big deal for people to realize they're [queer]. I hope that people get that it's just part of you, that it's accepted. Some people are [queer] and some people aren't and that's just understood and fine either way. I want it to be less of a big deal. I think we're getting there."

FOUR: **RESETTING EXPECTATIONS**

Permission to grieve, granted! Just do it without Baby Girl. One of the tallest hurdles parents face is grieving and resetting their expectations. It's alright to feel a sense of loss when realizing that life events you pictured, like a wedding, might look different than you previously thought. Barbie & Ken is now Barbie & Jen. The cake topper just got a bombshell upgrade!

Most parents don't realize these internalized expectations, so it can be a surprise to feel sad about it. Congratulations on being perfectly human. Whip out the Ben & Jerry's, Bridget Jones, the important thing is to grieve the future that will not happen. Give yourself space to move forward, then get excited for the new possibilities that can come from this reset. Having a queer daughter is full of many unexpected joys! Open your heart in order to embrace them as they come.

Conversely, just because your daughter is queer doesn't mean the trajectory of her life has changed. Unless she wants to join Gal Gadot on Themyscira (y'all seen Wonder Woman, right? If you haven't, it's going at the top of your homework list.) She can still fall in love, seek higher education, cultivate passions, grow a career, get married, and start a family. And be loved, accepted, and thrive in this beautiful world. Just because she's queer doesn't mean any of these things have to change unless she wants them to. The choice is hers.

Resetting expectations is difficult. However, it can be the difference between knowing your daughter the way America knows Oprah vs. deeply *knowing* your daughter as only you can.

FOLLOWING IN YOUR FOOTSTEPS

You may have always dreamed of your daughter attending your alma mater, joining the same clubs or having the same interests. Legacy has historically been presented as the passing on of one's identity. While baby girl Susie-Q might very well rush your sorority and become a mini-me or score the lead in the musical just like you did, she might also find that she feels more comfortable forging a different path. Listening to her WHY is very important. Her comfort, safety, and ability to gain confidence with peers in safe spaces is crucial. This doesn't mean she won't come back toward your interests later in life, but also remember that your daughter doesn't need to do everything the way that you did in order to bring value to your experiences.

Your college, while it might be a family tradition or a top-notch education, might not be the ideal environment for her to flourish. She has more to consider within this decision.

And now, consider **a relevant anecdote from Alex Kenworthy...**

I went to Baylor University located in Waco, Texas. (SIC'EM Bears!) and had a phenomenal collegiate experience. I loved my classes and my professors, I felt at home amongst peers with big goals who wanted to learn. I studied abroad and rushed a sorority. I still have a few best friends that I consider sisters. I stormed the field, the court, and I partied responsibly (contrary to Baylor's squeaky-clean reputation.) I consider myself a Christian, and I was amongst Christians.

But here's the kicker: During that time, I didn't know that I was gay. That ignorance gave me the bliss to LOVE this school and consider it a blessing. However, would I have gone there if I knew I was gay? Probably not.

I recently had a conversation with a mother whose daughter is a sophomore in high school and has come out. The mother would love to send her daughter to Baylor. My two cents: If it were my daughter, I would not send her there.

The student body as a majority comes from a locale that leans into strong political and religious beliefs, and humans have a way of putting others down. This environment will not build her up, love her huge, and accept her for who she is.

College is a time to explore education, friendships, independence, beliefs, politics, and activities. It's an experience that lays a foundation for who you are going to be. Judgment from your peers and your community can destroy this opportunity for becoming.

You may try to convince yourself that the school you want your daughter to attend isn't that harsh, and that the experience you had there was so wonderful that the good outweighs the bad, but don't let your own feelings blind you to the different set of circumstances your daughter is taking into her educational environment. This applies to high schools, colleges, graduate programs, etc. There is no institution, no matter how hands-off, that shouldn't be evaluated from this new perspective.

Placing your daughter in an accepting environment is vital to her future happiness.

DATING

First things first: **The greatest desire for your daughter is for her to be happy, which can look so many ways. Capiche?**

In the current culture, so much emphasis is placed on sex acts to define your sexual orientation. We want to bust up this preconceived notion for you. As you know from your life, there is so much more to it than that. When your daughter develops feelings for someone, it can come with all the same butterflies, electricity, initial crush, excitement, and chemistry that you experienced in your life.

Now, when it comes to stereotypes, let's blow the doors off...

Loneliness–Many parents assume that when their daughter comes out of the closet she is destined for a life of loneliness. This is because the cultural representation of queer women remains limited. It may seem, that there aren't many options for your daughter in our society to thrive. We're here to tell you that this is a bold-faced lie. A lie, we tell you!

Each major city has a thriving gay community, and that includes queer women... They come in hordes, hordes of queer women! In embracing her identity, she will be the opposite of lonely because she is joining a vast, vibrant, community. A community that makes her feel seen.

They may not be as visible to you, but they are there. Your daughter will have plenty of fish in the lady sea to choose from. She will learn, just like the rest of the world, through the trials and turmoil of dating whom she wants to share her heart with.

"Types": If your daughter is feminine, this doesn't dictate that she will date someone masculine or vice versa. Contrary to cultural beliefs, there is no binary "the boy one" and the "girl one" in the relationship. They're both girls! Your daughter could also be attracted to someone who is non-binary or trans, and the same thinking applies.

There is no right type for your daughter except for the type she is attracted to and connects with, and there is no predicting that. The only way to know is when she introduces you to someone special to her, which can even change from relationship to relationship.

Commitment: Just because your daughter is attracted to women doesn't mean she will want to commit immediately. There is an old lesbian stereotype called U-Hauling, meaning they move in together fast and early on. Your daughter might, but this is just as likely as it is with heterosexuals. Women in relationships fall on the same spectrum as straight people regarding how quickly they would like to commit vs. how commitment-phobic they are.

Again, when it comes to understanding how serious your daughter's relationship is, this will be something you have to hear from her and can't predict based on stereotypes.

Marriage: It is an old stereotype that gays don't want to get married. Don't all humans love when others tell them how they should live? Shut it, George. We're just trying to love each other until the day we die, what do you care?!

Now that gay marriage is legal across the United States, the number of LGBTQIA+ marriages is climbing. Being married to each other is the single greatest gift of our lives. We permit you to "awwww!" Your daughter can be a part of this trend, or not, if she doesn't want to be. The lovely reality is that now, it is her choice.

Having Kids: The stereotypes go both ways when addressing queer women wanting kids. The generalized stereotype of "gay people" is that they don't want kids, and the other stereotype is that queer women are constantly obsessed with having kids. Being queer does not determine whether one wants to build a family. That is just silly.

Speaking of family, let's dive into relationships…

Don't just assume that someone your daughter is dating is called her "partner." While many still use the term, this assumption makes us feel like your old-timey great-aunt whose "best friend" was just her "roommate." We see you, Great Aunt Betty. Whenever Papa Kenworthy calls Alex Ritter my partner, I feel like we're about to saddle up to herd cattle.

Let your daughter tell you the title of the person she is in a relationship with. That could be a partner, girlfriend, spouse, wife, etc. The important thing is not to assume you know based on outdated stereotypes, and instead listen to her and respect her answer. When you come from a good place, it's hard to go wrong. You are learning and doing your best, and there is so much grace and understanding for that.

Queer dating is a different ecosystem, and while I'm sure you've heard several tropes about women who date women, keep these notions out of conversations with your daughter as they pertain to her dating life. It's important to remember that your daughter is a unique individual, as are her romantic partners, so give her the dignity of informing you about these situations.

It's also possible that your daughter came out to you while dating another girl. If so, do not presume she will "go back to normal" if they break up. Her identity is not attached to any one specific person, and she is queer whether she is dating a girl or not.

One true difference between straight dating and queer dating is that the lines between dating and friendship can get particularly blurry when women date women. It can be emotionally intense and create a vulnerability that can be confusing. Allow your daughter to have these complex feelings and hold off on presuming your straight wisdom applies. If you venture into conversations around dating, ask her about her experience! If she's comfortable sharing, then she will share. Grab the popcorn, and go along for the ride with...

An anecdote from Alex Ritter...

When we met, I was still new to dating women, while Alex Kenworthy wasn't. I had lived in Los Angeles for a long time, but Alex Kenworthy had just moved to this city. While we felt a connection right away, we had different ideas about what we were looking for during this period. This led to an extended "Are we dating, or are we trying to protect a friendship?" It took about six months on that roller coaster to get on the same page and commit to being girlfriends. Both of our friends were equally exhausted.

And yes, two queer girls can be just friends. Just because your daughter is hanging out with another queer girl, or a group of queer girls doesn't mean she is interested in any of them. In fact, finding a group of queer friends is normal and should be encouraged. The queer community is so crucial after coming out.

GROWING A FAMILY

Real talk: There are options for growing a family that you might think are weird or unconventional. Beyond the method as old as time (adoption), there are different avenues for your daughter to start a family of her own. If you think this is weird, you should talk to your therapist and get over that. You don't have to understand every step someone takes to respect it.

However, not everyone may respect your daughter on the level she deserves. You must treat your future family with love and support and validate them like any other 'normal' family in this unsupportive world. A family is built from love, and the parentage of the children or how they came into the world is irrelevant.

If other people think her family is weird, they are behind the times. Tell Edith from your bingo club to mind her own beeswax.

HANNAH'S STORY

Our friend Hannah is from a Jewish household in San Diego, California.

"I grew up with compulsory heterosexuality–I presumed by default that I was straight. I never felt "don't be gay" or "I can't be gay," it just never occurred to me. I have found guys attractive, but I had zero desire to act on it."

"Honestly, the algorithm figures out you're gay before you do. My Discover page on Instagram was so queer."

"My "holy shit, I'm gay" moment wasn't until [my late 20s]. I told my brother first. It was a chill and thoughtful conversation, which I knew it would be. I was more worried about my sister's reaction because she was uptight about certain things in the past, but she was very supportive. She was more bummed that I thought she wouldn't be okay with it."

My mom had asked me if I was gay once before, and I said I wasn't. I wasn't lying, I just wasn't aware yet. So when I did come out her reaction was "why didn't you tell me?" It took me a while to be aware of it, and then it had to be real enough for me to say something about it. It wasn't like I was closeted."

"I came out to my parents over Passover. I was really nervous. Their initial reaction was, "Wait, are you serious?" When I said "Yes," they had questions. Now I know they were just trying to understand it."

That's why I first came out by saying, "I'm dating girls," and not labeling myself because I wasn't exactly sure where that fell yet, and then it was eventually: "Yes, I am a lesbian."

I could tell my parents were trying to understand what it all meant. My dad was concerned for my well-being and how being queer might make my life harder. They had questions about whether or not I wanted the same things. To get married, have kids, date Jews. I said yes to marriage. I feel strongly [in favor of] adoption, so since I'm not birthing children, there's no clock on it. And when it comes to dating Jews, it's a bonus but not a requirement.

"The chiller the branch of Judaism, the more progressive they tend to be. There are queer temples. My mom has lesbian friends at temple. Jews don't have a concept of hell, so queerness didn't come up in my religious education. My understanding of being gay was more societal. The attitude from society was less that being gay was wrong but that it was "weird."

"When I came out to my hetero roommate, she was the 65hilliest. I was afraid to tell anyone who had been my roommate because I didn't want them to think I had feelings toward them. But to them, it was just new information. It was a non-issue."

"When I was young, I skewed very Tomboy. Then when I got to middle and high school, there was this idea that I needed to be more feminine. I learned from the culture's perspective that feminine was good for girls and masculine was not."

"I had my friends, but I could feel the ecosystem around me. There were the jocks, the cool kids, places you didn't want to sit at lunch. The kids who fell at the top of the popular hierarchy fell into very old-school heteronormative types. Being gay was just never talked about much. There was a Gay/Straight Alliance on campus, but it never broke through, socially."

"I didn't know many gay people. If I did, they were guys. I had a lesbian Rabbi at my temple, but I didn't see myself in her and didn't relate to her. But in college, when I heard that a girl was bisexual, I was endlessly fascinated by her."

"Even though my parents were supportive, my dad didn't get why I had to be "lesbian Hannah" and lead with it in my identity. But it's who I am, where I feel comfortable, and it's also my community. They thought I was "performing the idea of lesbian," which I felt insulted by. When my dad asked, "Why do you have to be SO gay? Why do you have to make it your personality?" Deep down, I realized he was coming from a place of worry. He was worried that this could be detrimental to me in some way, put me in danger, or limit my opportunities. It was a process for me to understand him because it came across as very judgmental at first. I called my parents out on it and asked, "Hey, do you understand why this is not cool?" And they usually listened. ``

It was a nice gesture when they made an effort to go to San Diego Pride. It showed that they were in my corner for my happiness and trying to be understanding. They weren't going to second guess me for the rest of my life."

ADVICE FOR PARENTS WHOSE DAUGHTERS ARE COMING OUT?

"My mom told some people without asking me first if I wanted to be the one to tell them." So, avoid doing that.

"Listen to what your kid is telling you about their identity and where they are at."

"Ask questions with the aim of understanding, and then listen."

"Show your support with your willingness to learn. You don't have to understand something completely in order to respect it. You don't have to know the inner workings of how a person's sexuality or gender is for them. It's so nuanced; even among individuals in the community, it varies greatly. You don't have to interrogate them. This is just a facet of them, it isn't the whole thing. You don't have to treat someone differently because of it or have it at the forefront of your mind constantly. It's normal. We're all just people."

"Find avenues to educate yourself on queerness. The internet is your friend. While there are a lot of chaotic internet people, there are also eloquent speakers who break down and talk about different topics. Like Alok Vaid-Menon, for example."

"Don't try to claim personal experience of this community. Understand what is and isn't yours to speak on. You can cite things you've learned, but you can't speak for queer people or try to define them or pigeonhole them."

FIVE: **WHAT'S NEXT**

Now that we've covered the opening moves... What's next?

If you're a parent who has gone full rainbow in response to your daughter's announcement, this is awesome. However, everyone else might not be as gung-ho as you. Unfortunately, there are many boring people out there who still suck. Saying something like *"Everybody's gay these days"* or *"Why does that person bother you? You should be lucky to have such accepting parents,"* isn't helpful when your child faces rejection or judgment. Even if you are thinking these things. **In these moments, she needs you to be her ally and stand up with and for her.**

Here's the hard truth: the world is not an all-accepting place. Your daughter will not always be in spaces with accepting humans. It may be tempting to keep your daughter safe by telling her to *"dress less gay"* or *"straighten it out,"* ... but those aren't solutions. Try to refrain from pushing your daughter back into the closet to keep her safe. It is entirely acceptable to talk to her and coach her about being aware of her surroundings. You should trust your gut about what you must do to protect your family and discuss varying situations with your daughter. If someone says or does something inappropriate, make it clear that you will not tolerate their behavior or opinions around your daughter. You should also tell security and/or potentially leave the establishment. Sticking around for a concert, sporting event, etc., isn't more important than your daughter's safety. The Steelers are going to lose anyway.

Your daughter is going to be braver than you thought possible. She will also need to be aware. That is the reality.

COMING OUT TO FAMILY

Now, the predominant advice is to let your daughter tell other family members before you do. This allows her to control her story and share that vulnerable moment with those she trusts. However, there may be a situation in which your daughter would prefer you tell someone first, which is okay if you get her permission beforehand.

Other parent(s): If your daughter has come out to you solo, there could be another parent or stepparent she needs to come out to. Feel awesome about being the favorite, then ask her if she would like you present. Though it may be tempting to get ahead of it and tell your spouse, allow her the dignity of sharing this moment with them. Spilling the beans is a party foul. These can be cherished memories, after all.

Siblings: It is possible, and very likely, that your daughter has already come out to her siblings, especially if they're close. You may feel like you need to talk to them about it. This is another instance in which keeping the language based in love is important because children often model a reaction based on their parents. If you explain to a sibling, especially a younger sibling, that this is a huge deal and something to be worried about, they will be worried. However, if you explain that this new information is natural and doesn't change anything about their sister, your other children will likely understand faster than most adults.

If you're worried about confusing young children, you can relax. We know straight parents who have explained to their kids that "some kids have a mom and a dad, some have two moms, some have two dads…" and they understand better than most adults because it is simple. Humans aren't born casting shade, we learn it.

Grandparents: This can be a tricky one. By now, you can guess that telling her to "wait until grandma dies" would communicate that she has a shameful secret, so try to avoid that language.

Ask her what she would like to do and why it is important. We don't want to give any advice that would break up a family, but we want to help you remember that your daughter living truth is her right. She may want you in the room to tell them or she may want to do it on her own.

We understand that grandparents are tricky because they may come at your parenting skills, which can sting. You want your parents' approval as much as your child wants yours. In this instance, there couldn't be a more noble reaction than standing by your child. If her grandparents can't see that, they may need time. It's hard to turn a cruise ship. If this is the case, don't force closeness to convince Grandma to come around. It should be up to your daughter in which instances she wants to be around grandma, whether that be family events, birthdays, holidays, etc. Life is too short to spend Mother's Day brunch with a side-eye.

Extended family: Your daughter may not feel the need to come out to them and instead let the grapevine handle that. There is no rule that you have to come out to every person in the entire world, so whatever your daughter feels comfortable with should be good for you.

COMING OUT TO THE COMMUNITY

After coming out to family, the next step could be coming out to your greater social communities. It is important that you stand by her in her choices as to when, how, and who to come out to. The usual. We're breaking this record like it's our first Fletcher vinyl.

You should also discuss how you should handle conversations that come your way without her present.

Parents won't typically address a younger person in a community directly with their opinions about their sexuality. Still, if they do, your daughter can respond herself or bring you into the conversation. If she brings you in, stand by her over the opinion of those bringing their feelings to her doorstep. Let them know there isn't any room to triangulate you onto their side, and you will not entertain their opinion. Whether your daughter is present or not, it's important in conversations with other adults that you take her side and communicates that an opinion other than love and tolerance will not be accepted.

If those around you have alternative beliefs based on religion, etc. A good 'ol chestnut to hand them is that while they are entitled to their opinion, they are not entitled to share it with you or your daughter. This is your boundary, and if they cross it, you will consider removing them from your life. Their potato salad sucked anyway.

Each community is different, and you should discuss with your daughter how safe she is coming out to your greater social spheres, neighborhoods, religious communities, bowling league, etc. The emphasis should be on her safety first, and if she feels like she could be in danger of shaming or bullying, then now is the time to start reevaluating your connection to this community.

We know this can be a tough pill to swallow. Community is one of the centerpieces of the human experience and vital to our overall happiness and purpose. But do you really want to be a part of a community that will turn on your daughter for being honest about herself?

You may lose some people, but more people will surprise you in the most positive ways.

An anecdote from Alex Ritter...

One of my best friends is a Catholic school teacher, and I was terrified that she would no longer be my friend when I came out. I was afraid she'd fire me as a bridesmaid in her upcoming wedding. Boy, I couldn't have been more wrong. When I told her, she took my hand and told me how much she loved me, and I could tell that I hadn't changed at all in her eyes. She was sad that I thought she would judge me, and we've grown even closer since this experience. I'm not crying, you're crying!

Conversely, you may also be thinking: My community is so accepting, there's no problem here. If that's the case, hell yes! Even so, being different always comes with a microscope. No matter how accepting your community is, your daughter coming out could still be gossip-worthy, and this extra level of attention could still cause discomfort and require you to put up boundaries.

Talk to your daughter about how she would like this message to the community and what level of attention she is comfortable or uncomfortable with. Some children relish being lauded for their bravery, while others may not want any attention and to be treated like everybody else.

Unfortunately, there may be some people who will surprise you in a negative way with outdated opinions. This can feel like a betrayal because you expected better of them, but it is up to you to communicate your disagreement and stand steadfast in your support for your daughter. Holding firm on these boundaries of not accepting negativity will help exhibit your values to these people and allow them to come into alignment with yours. Once they get used to it they'll probably act like they never thought it was weird in the first place (this is common.)

COMING OUT AT SCHOOL

This can be nerve-wracking. Listen to your daughter's perspective on the situation, her classmates, the teachers, etc., and gauge how safe she feels coming out to a few close friends, her whole class, or the whole school.

The most important element to discuss is her safety and ensuring that she is not in danger of bullying or violence from judgmental administrators, other students, a cliquey friend group, or a disgruntled ex-boyfriend.

Where your daughter attends school and what type of school it is will inform this decision.

If she attends a religious school with a strict stance on LGBTQ+ issues, you may need to get ahead of it with the administration. Meet with them to firmly communicate that you will not tolerate your child being shamed or spoken down to by the adults in this establishment. They may respond appropriately at the moment, but this doesn't always mean it is an accepting place. Later there could be more questions about if the environment is healthy for her growth and self-esteem. Will she be allowed to stay on the soccer team? Will she be allowed to bring a girlfriend to prom? Will she be subjected to anti-LGBTQ rhetoric in theology classes? There could be ripple effects of this school's value system influencing how other students treat her, and it is important you give her the channel, to be honest with you about this if it gets bad. However, your message to the administration should be that you will not tolerate your daughter being bullied, and if she is, this will become a bigger problem for them. Respectfully, of course.

If your daughter attends a public school in a conservative area, you should still get ahead of it with the administration. There are laws in different states regarding what public educators are supposed to report to parents, along with their suggestions on how to handle the matter. It's possible they could react dramatically at the moment. All these things considered; it is better if the administration acts from a place of knowledge rather than surprise. Then the focus of the conversation can be about keeping this a safe environment for your daughter and being vigilant of bullying.

Even if your daughter attends a public school in a liberal area, friend groups and ex-boyfriends can still get their panties in a twist about how this changes their social dynamics. In this case, the bullying can be discreet. If so, it is important to keep the administration abreast of the situation so they can be on the lookout for malicious actors. However, most of the strife in these situations will come from complex social dynamics. Your daughter may need to expand her circle or take an interest in new activities with new people who didn't know her so well before she came out.

The final option: Everyone can surprise you! In response to your daughter's coming out, her school may decide to celebrate Pride, or she may get crowned prom queen. Nowadays, any of the above is possible, and preparing yourself for all possibilities is a good idea.

ONWARD...

If your daughter is being bullied, it may be challenging to decide how to respond, but this is a decision you should make together. The best thing you can do is continue to listen, and if she tells you she wants to leave a school, church, or her cousin's bar mitzvah, help her accomplish that.

If she is the only queer person in an environment, she will likely feel claustrophobic and anxious. This level of loneliness can have negative consequences.

JAMIE & KAYLA'S STORY

Jamie and Kayla are sisters. Jamie is a lesbian and two years younger than her straight sister, Kayla. They are our lifelong family friends from Colorado.

Jamie opened the interview by addressing her sister...

"Kayla, I can't thank you enough for being exactly who you are and loving me for exactly who I am." Jamie elaborates, "She's my closest confidant, my rock. She loves me unconditionally, and she puts up with all my antics. She's the best friend I've ever had or will have."

It's safe to say that they are close.

Kayla responds, "I can't even add to that because the feeling is so much the same. Jamie is the most important person in the world to me."

Kayla continues, "We played well and never fought when we were little. We were close, but we drove our mom *absolutely* nuts."

When turning to the subject of Jamie coming out, it wasn't straightforward. Jamie explains, "My sister and mother thought I was gay in high school."

Kayla adds, "Jamie, you had a friend in high school that you held hands with all the time. Either Mom or I said, "You two are close. Do you have romantic feelings towards her?" It was so not a thing; it was a casual ask. But then you were like, "What the hell is happening? No... are you suggesting that I'm gay??"

Jamie was clearly upset at the suggestion, so my mom and I were just like, "never mind."

Jamie explains, "My realization of being gay hadn't occurred to me at all at that point. I thought I was so straight. But [credit to] our mom, she's never felt any sort of homophobia."

Kayla adds, "In high school, I realized I could think for myself (outside what I was messaged about being gay in elementary school). I don't remember ever feeling anti-gay, but it was what we were taught, so it was strange."

"Jamie dives into her coming out story. "It all came up for me in my sorority. I met my friend... (we'll call her Emma), and I fell deeply in love with her, and even then, it took while for me to be okay with it. For a while, I thought, "Maybe I'm just in love with this one girl." I was holding out hope for forever... but I'm so gay."

When asked why it was so difficult to accept, Jamie considers, "It was a whole crisis. This wasn't the life I had imagined for myself. At the time, I thought, "I just can't believe that this is what this is, that this is what these feelings are." Emma wasn't out. She isn't to this day. Everything was in secret."

"The tipping point for every queer person is: What do you do now that you know you are this way? When I was dating women, I realized how much happier I was because I always felt like I was putting on a facade with the frat boys."

We asked Jamie once she knew that she was gay, what was the next step? "It cost me one of my best friendships because I was lying so much. And even at one point, my friend was like, "I know you're lying," and I was like, "I know that I'm lying too."

She asked why I wouldn't just tell her the truth, and I told her, "I can't." This was because it would've also outed Emma, who was determined to stay closeted.

When asked what it was like coming out to Kayla, Jamie responds, "I knew she'd be fine with it because she was fine with the idea when she and my mom brought it up in high school when I was 16."

Kayla jumps in, "Okay, so now we're talking about this. I've known [you were gay] since you were born. It's not a choice."

Jamie remembers, "I guess I did want to kiss all the girls in preschool. I wanted to be their husband."

Kayla rolls her eyes. "But you didn't think your sister knew...."

We move on to the topic of their youngest sister, Avery, who is ten years younger than Jamie.

Jamie explains, "When Avery was about thirteen, I said, "Don't be weirded out, but I'm a lesbian." Avery said, "Okay." I then asked her, "do you know what that is?" and she said, "yeah." I asked her if she was cool with it and she said, "yeah... can we go back to dancing now?" We'd been having a dance party."

Kayla chimes in, "See, even Avery knew."

Jamie continues. "I came out to my mother when Emma came home with me for Christmas. It was going to be obvious. My mother was lovely. She said, "God made you as perfect as you are." She knew that it wasn't a choice. I knew she'd be accepting in general. What upset me is that she told me not to tell Avery for a while."

Kayla replies, "Oh, I didn't know that, so I probably told [Avery]. She knew. We all knew."

We turn the conversation towards Kayla. Were there times she ever had to defend her sister for being gay? "Yes, people in the world make homosexual comments or jokes. My experience has been in telling them to sit down because I am going to educate you right the f*ck now."

Kayla continues, "Once, I'd fought with a friend who was newly religious, and she'd said homosexuality was a sin. She spewed Bible verses at me, and I spewed Bible verses at her. The last thing I'd ever said to her was that I would never have her standing next to me and my sister at my wedding."

Jamie adds, "Kayla has always been a huge protector."

Kayla continues, "No one has ever said anything negative to me about Jamie because I mean… they would no longer be here."

Jamie interjects, "There was this one time you told me about, when you were getting your nails done, the woman said something homophobic, and you refused to ever go back."

"Oh, yeah. I was so mad. I got up mid-messed-up nails and was like, never again motherf*cker, learn yourself some sh*t."

WHAT ADVICE DO YOU HAVE FOR SIBLINGS OF BABY GIRLS COMING OUT?

Kayla: It's your responsibility to shield your sibling from any hate. It's your responsibility to communicate to the rest of the family that (judgment and shame) is not right. The person who has come out and is their most vulnerable truest self isn't then responsible for making sure that other people in the family are *okay. It's up to the straight sibling to call people on their BS if they don't react well. Then, the other half of it is just to be there. To ensure your sibling feels loved, cared for, and accepted."*

SIX: GROWING TOGETHER & LOVING EACHOTHER

ENCOURAGING YOUR DAUGHTER TO FIND QUEER COMMUNITY

Now that you've learned so much about your daughter and her identity, it can be tempting to ask her why she needs a community of gay people. You've cultivated safe spaces for her at home and school and encouraged her to seek out accepting environments, so why does she need a different support system outside the mainstream? Aren't you cool enough for her??

It's fantastic that you've come to accept your daughter as being human, just like you! However, just like any other cultural group, there is a uniqueness to queer culture that is meant to be shared in community. Being queer is more than sexuality, it is culture and identity. There are trends, inside jokes, highs, and lows that are specific to your daughter's queer experience, and no one understands those particular pieces of her like others in the community. And that is okay! You are not meant to personally relate to every single moment and corner of your child's life. That would be exhausting. For the facets of her life where you can only offer empathy, encourage her to find community.

As you can see from every chapter of this book, we have many queer friends. They are our second family.

WHY PRIDE IS IMPORTANT

As an extension of the previous point, you may also wonder why, as a fully accepted human being, your daughter gets so excited about a parade. (Besides the fact that it's more fun than crowd surfing at a Taylor Swift concert. Or better yet, it's like crowd surfing on a bunch of Taylor Swifts.)

Here's the deal: The Stonewall Uprising, which protested homosexuality laws, is just over 50 years old. This is a drop in the bucket in the vast history of human rights. Unfortunately, there are still pockets of the world that see homosexuality as illegal or simply a negative attribute. So pride has always been about rejecting that shame and shoving that rainbow as high up in the sky as possible.

Our community was criminalized and forced to hide in the shadows, so Pride is also an opportunity for queer people to meet the vast array of other LGBTQIA+ people out in the open.

Conversely, you may also ask yourself: As a straight person, can I go to Pride? Straight allies are more than encouraged to attend Pride events. You're welcome! This community welcomes you and your support of your daughter. You can go with your daughter, with a PFLAG group, or with other friends and family. However, have this conversation with your daughter in advance. No one wants to be on display to a bunch of family members while they get their flirt on.

FANNING HER FLAME

While your daughter dives headfirst into her new life as a confident, out, and proud woman, continue to fan the flame of her other interests and friend groups.

The gay community can be a wonderful solace and point of connection, however, it isn't immune to drama (just like any social group!), so if she happens to have a falling out in that community, or experiences a tough breakup, it is important that she has other quadrants of her life to bolster her self-esteem and give her a sense of belonging while the choppy seas calm. Nothing mends a broken heart like landing a dragon flip on your new skateboard. Okay, that might be an exaggeration... but it doesn't hurt to dive into your passions.

Everything she was interested in before she came out could still be a part of her, and she doesn't have to give up any endeavor because she is gay. However, if she was overcompensating and trying to appear straight in a straight world, give her the grace of allowing her to abandon activities she doesn't actually love. Personally, we both could've skipped Cotillion.

This also applies to appearance. If, once your daughter comes out, you see her closet filling up with beanies and Converse sneakers, don't assume she is going out of her way to "act gay" to fit in with the larger queer girl community. It can be tempting for parents to assume this, but instead of thinking that coming out is changing her, give her the benefit of the doubt. Now that she is out she feels free to be her authentic self, including with her clothing stylings, rainbow belt buckle and all. Let her explore this.

What's exciting is that human beings are never just one thing, even though our culture likes to tell us otherwise. We live in a society that tells us that a lacrosse player can't also love playing the piano, Dungeons & Dragons, or be interested in fashion. Keep telling your daughter that whatever lights her fire, you support her.

WHEN YOUR DAUGHTER STARTS DATING

This is a big one, and it is fair to feel all sorts of emotions about your queer daughter dating. You may not know how to talk to her about it, what terminology to use or what to ask. That's why you have us, your friendly gay gurus.

The first reminder we'll lay on you is, you guessed it... boundaries. Let her share what she is comfortable sharing, and when she tells you she doesn't want to talk about something, let it be.

Trying to keep up is hard. Dating is a rollercoaster. If she is open to talking, just ask if you have questions. She will thank you for your curiosity and respect, even if her face turns red as a tomato.

Okay, now brace yourself for some S.E.X. talk. We promise to make it quick and painless...

You may also incorrectly assume that sex between queer girls is STD-proof. That is not the case, and if your daughter becomes sexually active, she should get tested regularly. To the extent that you would with a straight child, encourage her to get tested when she needs to, for both her health and the health of her partner(s). We do know for sure though, that sex between women can't get you pregnant. So you can relax there. But that is all we will say about that because we're not doctors!

SEEKING OUT ACCEPTING ENVIRONMENTS

In 2023, no school or environment is candid about not accepting gay people, and if they are, run fast in the other direction. However, most environments put on a welcoming facade, and it takes educated questions and time spent in the environment to truly understand if your daughter will be accepted and not just tolerated, or worse, a project to change. Fun times.

Key phrases to listen for that point to a place being unaccepting...

"We accept all of our students, but LGBTQ+ couples aren't allowed at prom/sorority formal/debutante/etc." This really means that we will tolerate you being here (and gladly take your money) so long as you are exactly the same as everyone else, but any evidence of your queerness isn't acceptable. Womp.

"Love the sinner, hate the sin.": This old chestnut. There is so much to dig into with this phrase, but here's what you should keep in mind: It is impossible to love a person and believe that their expression of love could effectively be a sin. Sins are for atoning and changing. What those who say this phrase want is for your daughter to repent and reject her queerness and act straight. What they are trying to convey to your daughter is that she will only be truly included once she finds her way towards straight-ness. Though everyone may lead with love and smiles, this environment is toxic. Make a hard left out of this bummerville.

"All are accepted here, but we do not acknowledge same-sex relationships in the classroom (read: within the culture) of this establishment." Again, this means that we will tolerate you and accept your money, but we are policing your daughter while she is here, and anything deemed outside the strict norms will result in shaming or being outcasted. Consider this: Let's say your daughter wants to write a queer character into a short story for her creative writing class, or she wants to present on Eleanor Roosevelt in history. An institution with this policy can either force your daughter to change her presentation or dock her grade for not meeting the school's guidelines. Do you want your daughter to be put in a position like that in front of her peers? I didn't think so.

"We don't acknowledge or encourage others to acknowledge Pride here." This one seems less overtly unaccepting, but a place with a stance on this enough to state it isn't going to support your daughter in being her true self. It also means that this place attracts a community that feels the same way and will make your daughter feel like a nuisance for just trying to live.

These are just a few phrases you may hear from administrators as you investigate where your daughter should invest her time, education, spiritual growth, ambitions, etc. Still, by now you should get the gist as to what unsupportive language sounds like.

Additionally, some important data to seek out when evaluating healthy environments for your child is how many other queer individuals, or individuals from queer families, exist in this community. **It is important that your daughter is not the only queer person in this environment** or even one of a tiny handful. This is for several reasons: the first is that when you are the only type of something in a cultural bubble, you are inherently othered from the rest of the group. You have to filter what you say, you worry about making others feel uncomfortable or weirded out. However, when there are already other queer people embraced in this community, you can relax because you don't feel as under the microscope as you would otherwise.

LIFE IS CONSTANTLY EVOLVING.

What might confuse straight parents are environments that talk the ally talk, but don't walk the walk.

An environment can seem like a good fit, but then these places can show their true colors later. Don't fall asleep at the wheel, mom and dad!

The key here is to keep an open line of communication with your daughter and that no matter how ingrained you or the rest of the family get in this place, she can if she wants to leave. Forcing her to stick out a school year or a season or until a play opens can expose her to a damaging and potentially dangerous environment.

JULIANA'S STORY

Our friend Juliana is Brazilian. She was raised in Sao Paulo before moving to the American East Coast. Her family is Catholic.

"I grew up in Sao Paulo, Brazil. It's a massive city in the top five most populated cities in the world. My parents worked when I was growing up and are still together. I have one brother who is three years younger."

"Growing up, [the belief] was very much that gay is bad. My dad and his buddies would make homophobic jokes. If the topic was brought up it was in a negative light. Most people from Brazil are Catholic. My family isn't very religious, but (Catholicism) is cultural."

"I never had contact with (queer) people growing up. As a kid, I was into sports and so was my dad. We're all very into soccer in Brazil, so that's what I played. I always played with the boys."

"I dressed masculinely. People would think I was a boy. It wasn't about sexuality; it was about gender. People would misgender me on purpose and say things like, "Do you think you're a boy?" Then, after puberty, I started conforming. I didn't have any female friends, so I started dressing girly. Eventually, I found my way into the popular group. "

"I'm bisexual, so when I was thirteen and fourteen, boys would have crushes on me and I would entertain those. I never went home and felt like I was hiding myself."

"For a while, I had intense female friendships. I had a best friend I'd hang out with at school, and then we'd get home and Skype.

It was normalized in this popular group to have one close best friend. We would cuddle, and at sleepovers, she'd be like, "I want to sleep with Juliana!" and I would get really excited about that. Thinking back, that was such a sign, but I didn't think about it at the time."

"I left Brazil for boarding school in Massachusetts when I was fifteen. I was hyper-focused on playing soccer in college and being in the top percent of my class that I didn't really date. No one was out at my boarding school back then, but [students there] are out now. This [younger] generation is so much better about queer stuff."

"One of my friends from back home came out right before college. She invited me to gay clubs in Sao Paulo and I remember feeling, wowed in that environment. I felt something, but then I thought, "I'm happy enough with men. Why would I do something that my parents, mostly my dad, isn't going to like and create a [problem] when I'm happy enough with men." I told myself, "Just don't try the cake. If you never try the cake, you won't know how much you like it." But then, in college, a girl kissed me. At that moment, I was like, "Well, f*ck." It was a sudden realization that I definitely (was into girls too).

"The summer before senior year, I had an internship in New York City, which is when I tried the girl dating apps. A couple of other out, queer girls from my college were in New York with me. I was getting comfortable with who I was. It was a pivotal summer."

"When I returned to college, I started dating a freshman girl who had been out since high school. She was only a few years younger, but it made a huge difference with how normalized it *was for her age group. Her parents were super cool. Until then, I had only dated guys."*

"So... Now I had a reason to tell my family. When I told my mom, she was all, "Yay! Cool!" Occasionally, she'll use the wrong language to describe [LGBTQ+ people], but it's not on purpose. If you teach her what to say, she'll correct it."

"My dad was not happy. He sees himself in me. My dad is proud of me because I excel in school and sports. When we all went to dinner - me, my girlfriend, my mom, my brother, and my dad - it was the worst dinner ever, it was so awkward. My dad didn't open his mouth once. He didn't know what to do. Afterward, he told me, "I just don't accept it.""

"We ended up not speaking for three months. Eventually, he started talking to me as he got comfortable with the idea. He's still getting comfortable. My mom pushes him along. She's been my champion. She asks him, "What's the difference? Do you want to lose this relationship with your daughter?" Because I'm bisexual, my mom tells me that in his heart, he hopes I'll find a guy I like one day. But at the end of the day, he'll just be waiting."

"My dad is a big family guy. Giving me away at my wedding and being a grandfather are things that he's excited about. So, when I told him about my girlfriend, I understood that if I were to marry a girl, his whole vision of my life would look completely different. It's taken him a while to digest."

"My current girlfriend (let's call her Riley) presents as more traditionally feminine, and my dad is more comfortable with that. The way someone presents is significant to him. My girlfriend in college was crunchy granola. Riley is more

digestible to my dad. It isn't great. How someone looks shouldn't determine how worthy they are of respect."

"My mom says that now my dad talks about Riley and me to his friends. She says she's so happy with the progress he's made. He's decided he isn't missing out on a relationship with me because I like girls. I once told him that what he'd said hurt my feelings, and he apologized. I forgive him because I know that he's trying and showing improvement. As time passed, I'd mention more about my life, and since I'd act normal about it, he'd act normal about it. I've talked to him openly about marrying a woman. We joke about a wedding budget. At the end of the day, I know a wedding is something that he wants to do for me."

"(One of the things that's still hard) is that he says if I have children, he wouldn't be able to like the children that weren't biologically mine. I think that's bullshit, but he says a genetic baby of our family is the one he will love more. My thinking is: If you're going to be a dick to any of my kids, then I won't let you hang out with them. I'm sure he's not going to want that, so. You get all of it, or you get none of it."

SEVEN: **YOUR DAUGHTER IS UNIQUE**

"What if my daughter doesn't fit into this generalized coming out narrative?"

Then, you're screwed!

Just kidding. We wouldn't leave you hanging like that.

Everyone's coming out story is different with its unique circumstances. We're here to help you out with a few specifics...

COMING OUT LATER IN LIFE

If your daughter is older when she comes out, she will experience different questions and circumstances.

Since your daughter has come out at an older age, it may be tempting to think that this hasn't been part of her identity her entire life. Whether or not she has been aware of it, it has always been there waiting for her to discover.

It is possible that your daughter has known for years but has kept this part of herself hidden for fear of religious or cultural shaming. It is also possible that your daughter didn't come to her big rainbow epiphany until recently. The queer journey isn't always a straight line! Pun intended!

As we discussed in a previous chapter, sexuality is a spectrum. For many, understanding the breadth of that takes a minute. It's a journey that can be full of angst, but once you come out is filled with joy. After a lifetime of not living as her most authentic self, you may see her engulfed in her identity for a while.

You might wonder, "Jessica, do you have to be SO gay?" The answer is: yes, Mildred! This is because she's accepting a piece of herself that she hasn't shown the world or allowed herself to spend time with. These feelings are coming at her like a tidal wave, and she's just trying to ride it out. This version of her might feel self-involved, but you should allow her the time to feel this way. Can you imagine going through a second puberty in your 30s, 40s, or even 50s? Your answer is probably: no, thank you, please.

Speaking of puberty, having not dated as her true self in the past, these early stages come with the highs and lows most people experience as adolescents. Since your daughter missed out on that period of her life, she feels all of it now, which can be overwhelming. She will feel the dichotomy of being an in-control adult in one quadrant of her life and wildly euphoric in the other. It's jarring. You feel crushes for the first time. She will ultimately see this process as beautiful because she has finally found her place in the human race.

We want to let you into how your daughter feels so that you can understand that she hasn't been hiding from you as much as she's been hiding from herself. Many who come out later in life often bond about not understanding why they felt perpetually on the outside of life, wondering why no one made them feel the way their friends felt about the men they love. As you have read in interviews evolving into herself, experimenting with style, finding what feels true... after a lifetime of not engaging with this part of herself, it can take a while to find how she feels comfortable presenting in the world.

You might be filled with worry for your child and her stability. Still, you need to trust her as an adult to make the best choices for herself. This includes dating, friends, and physical appearance.

Since coming out later has its own questions and discussions attached, below is an additional list of...

PHRASES TO AVOID:

"Has your whole life been a lie?" Absolutely not. Her whole life has been a journey you've had a front seat to. This is the most recent step in this journey towards knowing herself, and she is clueing you in on this milestone.

"Why did it take you this long?" Just like writing this book or running a marathon, it takes as long as it takes, Susan! It's a myth that we all figure everything out about ourselves by the time we leave adolescence. One of the many joys of being human is that we are constantly in motion. We all get there in our own time.

"This isn't because of (ex-boyfriend or ex-husband)?" While this is an understandable question to ask yourself, do not ask your daughter this. Instead, we will answer it for you! The answer to this question is: no. No one person, or even a handful of people, can sway your daughter toward being queer. These people were part of her journey toward understanding her true self.

If you'd like some TMI, many queer women have had long-term relationships with men in which they thought the sex was just "fine" or even maybe they're just "a person who doesn't like sex," and those thoughts have carried her through all these years. However, as all of us who have had great sex know, 'fine' isn't what songs, novels and plays for thousands of years have been about.

You don't feel like this is a phase? It may be tempting to think that her coming out has something to do with where she is in her life and needing a change or new level of excitement (Be gay or take up windsurfing?). If your daughter is queer, it is a constant, and just because she is now acting on it after many years doesn't mean it is fleeting.

How do you know you're queer if you haven't had sex with a woman? I'm going to answer this question with a question: Did you know that you were straight before you had straight sex? You probably did. No one's sexual identity is defined by their experience, <u>and the fact that she wants to have sex with women is enough for her to know that she is queer.</u> We underlined that sentence because it is important. Let it soak in, Kevin!

NON-BINARY & TRANS BUDDIES

This section is only a primer for understanding your trans or non-binary child. Since this is not our lived experience, we recommend you seek out more knowledgeable resources.

However, we would love to be your first step in the right direction! Your child's sex assigned at birth may not adhere to their definition of themselves.

Although the word 'transgender' and our modern definition of it has only been used since the 20th century, people who would fit under this definition have existed in every culture throughout recorded history.

When your child comes out to you about their gender, this doesn't mean they are also coming out to you about their sexuality.

Regardless of someone's gender identity, they could be attracted to men, women, or both.

Gender and sexuality are different discussions. The human brain can hold more than one idea at a time–make space to discuss both and how they intertwine in your child's life.

EPILOGUE: ELLEN'S STORY

"The most important thing you can do is always tell the truth."

-Ellen (Alex Kenworthy's Mom)

Now that we've regaled you with a library on how to love your baby girl who likes girls, we want to end with a few words from Alex Kenworthy's mom, Ellen, who has come a tremendous way towards loving and supporting Alex.

We hope that you and your daughter come to the same wonderful, loving place that Alex and her mother have.

Below is their story...

When Alex Kenworthy first came out to her mom, all Ellen knew of being gay was that it was hard.

Ellen: I grew up in a Catholic community in small-town Louisiana. If there were any gay people around, we didn't know, at the time we didn't know much about homosexuality. However, when I was in high school, there was a guy all the boys treated badly and called him queer. It was disturbing. He worked on having a social life by focusing on his relationships with the girls in our class.

Then, at the age of twenty-three, I moved to Dallas. The company I was working for was based in Marin County, CA [outside San Francisco.] Almost everyone I worked with there was gay. I became close friends with most of them. At this time, these people were ridiculed, insulted, and had difficulty making friends outside of San Francisco. I particularly got close to the VP of Marketing, a wonderful gay man whom I adored. Unbeknownst to me, he contracted AIDS. I enjoyed a wonderful friendship with him, and I often think of him to this day. It was so sad; it broke my heart. There wasn't a treatment for AIDS then. This world lost so many intelligent, creative, loving people to that terrible disease.

My experience of a gay person's life was bullying, illness, and death. That fear presented itself when Alex told me her truth.

My life since the day Alex was born was one of fear of losing her. Alex was a preemie born of an emergency C-Section, which made me a very protective mother. Alex, I tried to keep you out of pain for most of your life. All I could think was that you were choosing to be gay, and that hurt me because I knew it meant a hard life. This world is difficult - full of hypocrites and violent people who don't understand. I can't make those choices for you; I can't take the hard things away from you. You always thought I was against you instead of being for you. I didn't understand why you thought I was there to interrupt what was good for you. Again, my heart was broken. But Alex, you set me straight, "it is not a choice; it is who I am... God made me this way, and He loves me."

For the longest time, we were missing each other. It was my hurt vs. your determination to be true to who you are. You were upset because you didn't get the reaction from me that you wanted. I was shocked. I didn't have time to wrap my head around it. I was worried that you would be driven from your faith because you had all these Christian friends who would disown you. I was trying to protect you from your peer group.

Until you told me about your sexuality, our relationship was strained, and I didn't understand why.

In an effort to protect you, I came across as rejecting you.

Alex: You want your protectors to tell you that it's going to be okay. **There's a lot of light in the darkness of owning your truth,** and I feel like we missed each other on that. But through time, I saw you process and take steps toward me. I think about how you have come to show your love. You understand what my wife and I have.

You made many changes in your life to move towards me.

Ellen: I went to see a counselor. This helped me understand and develop a new relationship with you. As time passed, I saw it wasn't a new relationship with you, but a better one with you. Our relationship was so bad; we could barely talk. I needed counseling to understand. I realized your perception of me was that I was trying to take over your life and tell you who to be.

In addition to therapy, I changed churches. I talked to my pastor about his negative message regarding homosexuality. I think it's wrong. I think a lot of fear comes from people lacking education about these topics—they take an aggressive stance towards things that are different from them, but they don't think about the challenges Alex and I faced as a family. What families in his congregation were facing.

The Pastor at that church was not approaching the topic with love. I can't deal with people who can't think through their limitations, so I found a new church.

Alex: When I think of the message, "love the sinner hate the sin," which I heard from pastors in my life, I think, "you can't tell me that the purest love I've ever felt is a sin." No one will ever convince me that message comes from the God of love.

Thank you for moving towards me... You were so wonderful on my wedding day

Ellen: On your wedding day, I was very proud of you. You both looked beautiful. There was so much love there. That morning I asked if it was okay for me to check on Ritter. I knew her parents refused to be part of the wedding. I went into Ritter's room because I wanted to make sure she knew that she had a mother there for her too. She looked stunning.

Alex: That's a moment I cherish from that day. You came back in, I was getting my hair done, and you said with tears in your eyes "Wait till you see Rit, she looks so gorgeous, you are going to die." I felt so accepted and understood by you.

Do you have a message to share with the parents reading this book?

Ellen: My whole message has been, whether you're Christian or not, show love to one another. This world is such a lonely place to be a selfish and judgmental person. Listen, pay attention, and give lots of hugs. Until you stand in someone else's shoes you cannot comprehend what is happening in their life. Go walk in their shoes and then come back to me and tell me how you feel about it.

Acknowledgements

This book is a labor of love and would not have been possible without our family and friends who helped breathe its message into existence.

Ashley King, Elle Lipson, Ana Alvarenga and those who shared their stories. Your fierce support, technical prowess, and hours of inspired reflection have given this book its soul.

Malaya Lewandowski, Amy King, and Samantha Laird. Your honest feedback and years of loving support have changed lives.

To Ellen, thank you for participating with love and honesty.

To all the parents who came to us with open hearts wanting to learn how to love and support their daughters, thank you for inspiring us.

Citations

"Dr. Jane Rigby Named 2022 LGBTQ+ Scientist Of the Year | College Of Science." Dr. Jane Rigby Named 2022 LGBTQ+ Scientist Of the Year | College Of Science, 2 June 2022, science.arizona.edu/news/2022/06/dr-jane-rigby-named-2022-lgbtq-scientist-year.

"Sarah Paulson Talks the Aftermath of Coming Out and New Movie 'Carol' | KitschMix." KitschMix, kitschmix.com/sarah-paulson-talks-accidentally-coming-out-and-new-movie-carol.

Nast, Condé, and @VanityFair. "Aubrey Plaza Opens up About Her Sexuality." Vanity Fair, 9 July 2016, www.vanityfair.com/culture/2016/07/aubrey-plaza-sexuality.

"Actress Tessa Thompson Reveals She's Attracted to Both Men and Women." GAY TIMES, 1 July 2018, www.gaytimes.co.uk/life/actress-tessa-thompson-reveals-shes-attracted-to-both-men-and-women.

Setoodeh, Ramin. "Cara Delevingne on Her Pansexual Identity, Singing With Fiona Apple and What Pride Means to Her." Variety, 3 June 2020, variety.com/2020/film/features/cara-delevingne-pansexual-fiona-apple-pride-lgbtq-1234623248.

"Robin Roberts Is Gay: Thanks, Longtime Girlfriend in Facebook Post." Los Angeles Times, 30 Dec. 2013, www.latimes.com/entertainment/gossip/la-et-mg-robin-roberts-gay-lesbian-out-20131230-story.html.

"Margaret Cho Opens up About Her LGBTQ Identity: 'I Definitely Still Feel Like an Outsider.'" Yahoo Life, www.yahoo.com/lifestyle/margaret-cho-pride-190105189.html.

Nast, Condé, and @Allure_magazine. "Kate McKinnon Just Gave a Rare Speech About Her Sexuality at the Golden Globes." Allure, 6 Jan. 2020, www.allure.com/story/golden-globes-2020-kate-mckinnon-coming-out-speech.

"Coming Out 'Made Me a Better, Fuller Person,' Says U.S. Soccer Star Megan Rapinoe | CBC Radio." CBC, www.cbc.ca/radio/sunday/the-sunday-magazine-for-november-29-2020-1.5817667/coming-out-made-me-a-better-more-full-person-says-u-s-soccer-star-megan-rapinoe-1.5819650.

"Demi Lovato Shares About Her Sexuality: 'I Know Who I Am and What I Am.'" TODAY.com, www.today.com/popculture/demi-lovato-talks-about-her-sexuality-glamour-magazine-t211413.

"Lady Gaga Opens up About Her Sexuality." MTV, 28 May 2009, www.mtv.com/news/qnfrtq/lady-gaga-opens-up-about-her-sexuality.

"Lorraine Hansberry | Making Gay History." Making Gay History, makinggayhistory.com/podcast/lorraine-Hansberry.

Benton, Nicholas F. "The Secret of Eleanor Roosevelt's Success - Falls Church News-Press Online." Falls Church News-Press Online - Falls Church and Northern Virginia's Premier Weekly Newspaper, 18 Sept. 2014, www.fcnp.com/2014/09/17/the-secret-of-eleanor-roosevelts-success.

"Why Sally Ride Waited Until Her Death to Tell the World She Was Gay." NBC News, 25 July 2012, www.nbcnews.com/sciencemain/why-sally-ride-waited-until-her-death-tell-world-she-908942.

About The Authors

Alex + Alex are a married couple who grew up on the same street in Denver, Colorado but never crossed paths until their mid-20s at a famous gay bar, The Abbey, in Los Angeles.

Alex Ritter is a screenwriter, having written on SyFy's *The Magicians*. She is a member of the Writers Guild of America, West.

Alex Kenworthy has a successful career in Sales. She currently works in SAS and runs a team on the West Coast.

Together, their mission is to create content for queer women to see themselves reflected authentically in the world.

Connect with Alex + Alex:

@AlexAndAlexUniverse

@YourBabyGirlLikesGirls

AlexAndAlexUniverse.com